HOW GOOD IS MY PITCH DECK?

IGNITE YOUR STARTUP'S STORY AND ATTRACT INVESTOR CAPITAL

KEANE ANGLE

STORYPITCHDECKS.COM

DOWNLOAD THE FREE COMPANION KIT!

I've created a folder with several useful supplementary documents that expand on the concepts in this book.

Visit This Link To Download:
https://stry.pro/hgkit

Included in the kit:
Before-after pitch decks
One-page cheat sheets
Printable worksheets
Resources and links

INTRODUCTION

THE FOUNDER'S PITCH DECK DILEMMA

AFTER SPENDING the last two to three years working with hundreds of startup founders, I discovered they all share one thing. At some point, they all ask themselves the same question:

Is my pitch deck good enough to raise investor capital?

For many founders, creating a pitch deck is one of the most challenging parts of the fundraising process, and fundraising can be one of the most difficult parts of getting their startup off the ground.

What comes next is just as hard: finding investors to pitch. Some founders have pre-existing networks, while others come into it with zero connections.

Either way, founders need a fantastic pitch deck that sets them apart from the rest of the competition. The goal is to leapfrog from the big stack to the short stack of pitch decks that investors will consider.

STORY Pitch Decks, the pitch deck consulting firm I founded, has researched precisely this. We ran an in-depth survey of 300 active startup founders to understand the level of effort they put into their pitch decks.

Of those surveyed, 56% were male, 44% were female, and all were in the United States. Respondents ranged from 18 to 54 years old most between the ages of 25 and 44.

Half were founders on top of working full-time for another company, while the other half were full-time founders or free-lancers founding a startup.

At the time of the survey, 40% were raising investment funding while nearly the same amount (38%) had planned to raise in the next six months, with the remaining 20% aiming to raise in six months to a year.

To put this simply, every one of the 300 founders we surveyed was either currently raising funds or was planning to do so in the next year.

Regarding the funding sought, 70% of surveyed founders sought between $150k and $5 million, with the remaining seeking over $5 million.

Digging deeper, we asked them about the state of their pitch decks. Here's what we found:

   33% - We just started working on it, but it's not done yet

23% - We have been struggling for weeks or months to get it done

16% - Our pitch deck is done, and we're happy with it

15% - We have not started working on it yet, but need to

13% - We have a completed pitch deck, but we're not happy with it

Just 16% of founders said that they had completed their pitch deck and were happy with it. Based on this, it's evident that most founders (84%) struggle with creating a pitch deck with which they are comfortable and confident.

Founders feel personally responsible for making their pitch deck, and rightly so. Half the founders (56%) spent at least an hour or more each day on their pitch deck. That's a lot of time for a founder to spend on something.

Looking at these insights at a macro level has led us to conclude that founders need tons of help with pitch decks. Founders need to quickly and knowledgeably create a document that tells the story of their business in a way that investors will believe in enough to invest in. Startup founders can usually finish that first draft, but making it extraordinary is much more complex and amorphous.

That's why I wrote this book.

You're about to learn frameworks and strategies that I created exclusively for this book. I based these on my real-world experience helping hundreds of startup founders raise capital. By the end of this book, founders will be able to evaluate the strengths and weaknesses of their startup's story, boost the power of those elements working the hardest, and eliminate or mitigate the detracting parts of their story.

THE THREE PARTS OF THIS BOOK

1. **Evaluate Your Story**
2. **Elevate Your Positioning**
3. **Eliminate The Fluff**

Part One: Evaluate Your Story

First, I'll provide you with a framework to quantitatively understand which parts of your business are adding to the overall power of your story. I will also show you how to pinpoint and mitigate the biggest detractors of their stories. I call these two elements *boosters and draggers*. Boosters and draggers contribute to what I refer to as a *lift score* which is a quantitative evaluation of how compelling your startup's story is to investors.

Part Two: Elevate Your Positioning

Next, I'll give you another framework to understand how to ideally position your startup within an industry. As you might expect, the *storyline compass* will point you in the best direction possible and show you how to conquer that direction like no other in the industry. You'll also be able to use the compass for your entire business strategy, not just for your pitch deck. After that, you will know how to dial up each of the most important factors in your pitch deck to align with that direction. This process will sharpen all the messaging in your pitch around a single message providing much-needed focus.

Part Three: Eliminate The Fluff

Last, I'll show you how to eliminate unnecessary fluff at a macro and micro level within your pitch. In this final section, I'll cover the most common elements of a pitch that founders can often trim back at a high level and down in the details. I'll also show you how to handle investor feedback after you've presented your deck a few times.

After these three sections, you'll understand where you are now with your pitch, where you need to go, and how to get there.

"WHY SHOULD I LISTEN TO THIS GUY?"

Since I entered the workforce in 2007, my professional roles have always been about taking complex subject matters and communicating them in a way that is easy for most audiences to understand.

Before starting STORY Pitch Decks, I spent over a decade as a Fortune 500 brand advertising creative strategist. From 2007 to 2018, I helped global brands communicate effectively with hundreds of millions of people. During this time, my clients included Coca-Cola, General Electric, IKEA, NBC Universal, Burger King, Kraft Foods, Oscar Mayer, Procter & Gamble, Church & Dwight, Unilever, Diageo, Mattel, and more.

I also picked up a few ad industry awards, such as several Cannes Lions, a Webby, and a couple of Effies. Direct Marketing News also recognized me on their *Top 30 Under 30* list in 2010. On my last night as an ad strategist living in London, I took home an APG award for building one of the most innovative strategy teams in the United Kingdom.

For those unfamiliar with the advertising world (which is probably most of you), all a strategist does is create pitch decks to convince C-level executives to invest millions of dollars in an agency's advertising campaign ideas. So, I was a pitch deck specialist before I was a pitch deck specialist.

In 2018, I jumped out of advertising and became a full-time consultant, writing and designing presentations for companies like Mondelez International and Marriott Hotels Group. I also ran a presentation writing and designed a professional development program where I trained over a thousand Fortune 500 employees worldwide to create better presentations that get results.

In late 2020, I started STORY Pitch Decks and shifted focus to exclusively work with startup founders. Entrepreneurship is in my blood. I'm an entrepreneur, my mom is an entrepreneur, my dad's an entrepreneur, my dad's dad was an entrepreneur, and my wife is an entrepreneur.

One of the most satisfying things in the world to me is working with a brilliant startup founder doing something extraordinary but needs a little help telling their story to others clearly, compellingly, and concisely. Humans are storytellers, and there's real art and science behind it. Stories are how we learn about the world around us. Evolution hardwired humans for stories, and a pitch is a concise story. It's an elegant telling of why a startup exists. It also covers its past, present and potential future. It ends with what's needed to get to that new future.

Since 2020, my team and I have written and designed pitch decks for over 140 startups in early-stage rounds. Most startups we've worked with have been at the Seed and Series-A rounds. Our pitch decks have helped raise over a quarter of a billion for startups at a rate that hovers around 40%, forty times higher than the industry average of 1%. In total, I've spent well over 10,000 hours helping startups to tell their story in a way that wins the hearts and minds of investors. My team and I have also conducted numerous research studies on publicly available investor opinions to help better determine what they want in a great pitch deck.

Beyond working with startups, my team and I have helped raise billions in capital for venture funds and other investment vehicles, such as real estate and heavy industrial, energy, and transportation projects. We've also helped dozens of sales teams and organizations overhaul how they pitch their products and services to companies to boost their win rates.

Lastly, I spent over a year and a half as a fractional chief marketing officer for a language learning startup called Prismatext. In 12 months of operation, I drove the company's first six figures in revenue and provided the groundwork for a successful Pre-seed capital raise. Ultimately, I left Prismatext to focus on STORY, but my time working at a startup has been instrumental in helping to understand the mindset and real-world struggles of the clients I help every day.

A FEW ASSUMPTIONS ABOUT YOU

Expectation-setting time! I'd like first to lay out a few assumptions about you, your startup, and your pitch deck.

. . .

Assumption #1: You are a startup founder.

I will assume that because you picked up this book in the first place, you are a startup founder or co-founder. You're at the top of your organization regarding leadership and probably the one building your company's pitch deck.

Assumption #2: You are knee-deep in building your startup.

Next, I'll assume that you've been working on your startup for a decent period of time and have made good progress. From what I've seen, startup founders who've been working on their startup for at least a year are the ones who are best suited to create a compelling pitch deck that raises successfully. If you are a founder that has just had an idea and has yet to do anything about it, I recommend reading about entrepreneurship and getting a startup off the ground instead of reading this book. Instead, this book assumes that you have a clear idea of what your startup does, who it does it for, why it does it, and how it does it.

Assumption #3: You are building or have built a pitch deck.

The last assumption I'll make is that you are working on a draft of your pitch deck or are unsatisfied with the current version of your pitch deck. If this is the case, don't worry! You're not alone. This place is the most common headspace for startup founders working on their pitch decks. As such, this book will help you understand where your pitch is strong, where it's not so strong, and how you can improve it.

———

FOUNDATIONS TO HAVE IN PLACE BEFORE READING

I just mentioned that founders reading this book should have a few things already figured out. These things include:

1. Why your startup exists
2. What your startup does
3. Who your startup does it for
4. How your product or services work

Why Your Startup Exists

The most common ways I've seen founders answer this question are to solve a problem or achieve a mission.

I believe that every business exists to solve a problem, no matter what. So, I always answer this question using the first of the two above items. Horses solved the problem of having to walk everywhere. Bicycles and cars solved the horses and carriages issues. Taxis solved the problems related to cars and car ownership. Uber and ride-share services solved the problems with taxis. Electric vehicles solved the problems associated with combustion engines. And soon, on-demand vertical take-off and landing aircraft will solve the problems of cars and traffic congestion.

We can apply this concept to any category or industry. If you don't think that your startup exists to solve a problem, I highly encourage you to rethink this assumption. People pay to have their problems solved—even if that problem is "I'm bored and want to be entertained." If people don't think they have a problem, they won't be willing to pay someone to solve it.

Here's a quick story as an example. In late 2019, I started a company called Deliverable Coaching. The problem I thought I was solving was simple: employees who produce reports and plans in the form of presentations regularly are great at thinking and analyzing, but they could be better at packaging that information into a story. Specifically, my initial target was advertising agencies. So, I built an excellent learning and development program to solve this problem. The program was eight weeks long and it included flat per-participant pricing, and I even evaluated participants before and after to demonstrate results. Participants loved it, managers loved it, and my client's clients loved it.

However, there was a flaw in my logic. My target (advertising agencies) didn't think they had a problem with their client presentations. Ad agencies felt that they were already producing fantastic deliverables for their clients. As a result, my sales cycle was 4-6 months long, and new clients were hard-won. I was trying to solve a problem that *wasn't a real problem for my clients.*

Because of this, the fundamental principles I had founded the business on were flawed. So, I shut it down and began focusing on STORY Pitch Decks. My new audience and the problems I was solving for them (startup founders struggling to create an excellent pitch deck that lands funding) were very real and widespread among this audience. Once I nailed the problem, I did everything I could to understand it and then focused all of my company's efforts on solving it as best as possible.

Investors call this a product-market fit, which is what almost every early-stage investor is looking for in a company. Product-market fit is when a company's current product "fits" to solve a specific problem for one particular audience. Investors usually measure this state in the form of revenue growth over time.

That's my two cents on solving a problem. But what about a vision or a mission statement? Startup founders often have a phrase like this in their pitch deck:

We exist to install solar panels on one million new homes in the next five years.

OR

Our mission is to make the Earth healthier by transforming how Americans use solar power in their homes.

While both of these statements are good reasons to exist ethically, neither talks about the problem that the business solves for its target end-user; homeowners.

In the first example, why must solar panels be installed on a million new homes in the next five years? We've forced the reader to ask a second question after reading it. The reason (to reduce greenhouse emissions) is nowhere in that statement.

With regards to the second statement, it mentions "making the Earth healthier." Again though, this is a vague statement. What qualifies as a "healthy" Earth? How do we know if we've reached that goal? These and other questions would flow from your audience's mind as they read it. Again, this statement doesn't directly tackle the problem they solve for their target audience.

Looking deeper into these statements and what they're discussing (residential solar), we can uncover the end-user problem they solve by asking a few questions. Why don't more homes have solar panels on them already? Is it too expensive? Too confusing? Do they not know how to find providers in their area? Is there a massive educational gap in understanding what goes into a rooftop solar system?

These questions can pinpoint an underlying problem or problems within the industry that the startup can solve for its end-users. In other words, a moneymaking reason for the startup to exist would now be in investors' minds.

To wrap this section up, don't confuse the vision or mission of your company with the problem you solve for a given target or industry. Clear separation between these two crucial elements will go a long way to sharpening your startup's reason to exist.

What Your Startup Does

Knowing what your startup does is probably the most basic information a founder should articulate before doing anything. I like to start by defining the industry in which a given startup operates. For instance, enterprise collaboration software, weather satellite and data processing, peer-to-peer dating apps, or streaming entertainment content geared toward middle-aged men.

Naturally, humans like to put things in buckets. Investors, who are also human, like to put things in buckets so they know how to think about them. For startups, this bucket usually starts with picking an industry to operate within. Each industry or sector has its ways of conducting business, its supply chains, its leaders and innovators, and their market size (typically expressed as the total amount of revenue that all companies within a given industry bring in annually). More importantly, every investor usually has their favorite industries or industries they're at least interested in.

Before you say, "But we're totally unique and don't fit into any industry!" I've got a word of caution for you. Investors usually see startups that don't clearly define their industry (r competitors as having a product without a target audience to buy it. If there is no need, there's no problem. If there's no problem, there's usually no real short-term or long-term revenue potential to capture. Without this, there's no reason for an investor to invest because there's no stable, significant source of revenue that founders can capture to drive up the startup's valuation and earn a return on investment (ROI).

I like to think about industries as giant pizzas (bear with me here). The pizza represents the total revenue earned each year by all the companies within that industry. Each company gets a slice. Some companies have bigger slices than others. Sometimes half an entire pizza goes to a single company, while the other half is split among dozens of smaller companies. All the pizza must be eaten, and there aren't any extra or free slices just sitting there waiting for a new company to come along. No chefs are sprinting in from the kitchen saying, "Oh, here's an extra slice for you, dear newcomer." So when a new competitor takes a seat at the table, they usually take a bite out of someone else's pizza slice.

Both are hard to do, yet every successful startup has managed to do both.

Occasionally, pizzas become so big that *new* pizzas break off from the main pizza. Electric cars, for instance, are maturing as their own industry as nearly every major manufacturer rolls out new product lines to address this rapidly emerging market. Hopefully, this metaphor gave you an interesting perspective on how to think about your industry and target market.

For example, small market opportunities, anything under $1 billion, are something that many investors avoid. In large industries or market opportunities (over $100 billion, for example), a new entrant into this category has a greater chance of success due to the larger initial opportunity size.

Here are a few example industry sizes:

Global legal tech market: $8.2 billion market size by 2029 spread across lots of smaller companies and only a few major ones[1]

US online food delivery market: $22.4 billion in 2021 spread across a handful of major companies and only a few smaller ones[2]

US pet toys market: $678 million in 2020 spread across tons of major and minor players with no dominant companies[3]

Who Your Startup Does It For

If you know your industry, you can answer this question. For instance, if a startup operates in legal technology, it's safe to assume that law firms and legal teams will be your target audience or end-user. Yes, there are likely a few other layers of decision-makers and users in there, but lawyers are the ones who use legal software and technology. We could get even more specific and say that we built the solution for small and medium law firms or legal teams operating in the United States. This target could change, but for early-stage companies, it's best to focus on a single industry and audience.

Understanding your target audience is valuable in the case of pitch decks for two reasons:

1. When you understand your audience, you can understand their problems and build better solutions for those problems.
2. When you understand your audience, you can more accurately estimate a business's market size and revenue potential.

Addressing the first point is a fundamental element that every business leader should always consider. Businesses exist to solve problems for their customers. By understanding them more, businesses can build products, services, and experiences for them. In turn, this hopefully increases the value provided to that audience in exchange for buckets of cash.

Investors usually have high regard for founders that are actively listening to their target audience. The rationale behind this is that companies who are more dialed into the needs of their customers are more likely to succeed by creating things that their customers will want to spend money on.

We can calculate the total market opportunity for a startup from the bottom up: take the average annual spend per customer on your product or services and multiply that by the total number of individual customers in a given industry.

For example, if your startup's average annual contract value is $10,000 (actual or forecasted) and there are 5 million potential customers in a given industry and market, we would multiply $10,000 by 5,000,000 and get a $50 billion total annual revenue opportunity.

(Avg. Annual Customer Spend)

$\times$

(Total Number of Customers)

= TOTAL ANNUAL REVENUE OPPORTUNITY

Founders can adjust this formula for any business model or industry. In general, this is a good measure of a business's current and future growth potential, and it starts by knowing who your startup's customers are and how many of them there are.

How Your Product Or Services Work

The last and final fundamental element that I'm assuming founders have nailed down before reading this book is their products or services and how they work.

That means having answers to the following questions. If you do not have at least a rough answer to these questions written out, I urge you to press pause on reading this book and instead focus on defining your business a bit more.

What do you sell?

Can you articulate what you sell to earn revenue in one concise statement? For some companies, this is easy to answer (which is a good thing). For other startups I've worked with, this can be a real challenge to articulate. Regardless of where you stand on the issue, we'll sharpen how you talk about your product or services later in the book. It will be fine if you have a reasonable product description. Two important notes here. First, if you sell more than one thing, dial it back and focus on the revenue stream that will bring in most of your earnings over the next year or two. Second, try to avoid service-based business models that require your employee count to grow directly to your customer count. This operating model is an "unscalable" business and tends to be avoided by investors due to lower operating margins.

How do you charge for it?

The answer to this is your pricing and revenue model. Make sure it's simple and easy to explain. Investors prefer business models that allow startups to acquire a customer once and earn incremental revenue from them. Investors evaluate these models in a metric known as the CAC:LTV ratio, or Customer Acquisition Costs to Lifetime Value ratio. Investors usually want to see at least a 1:3 ratio, meaning that for every $1 you spent acquiring a customer, you earned at least $3 in revenue from them over their lifetime as a customer.

How much does it cost you to deliver?

This question also includes knowing your cost of goods sold (COGS), even if your business doesn't sell physical goods. Knowing this info is vital to early-stage firms because these metrics form the financial foundations the entire company will operate on for the foreseeable future. For pre-revenue businesses, this can be difficult to estimate. However, that doesn't mean founders should ignore COGS completely. Instead, these companies should, at the very least, estimate operating costs and expenses before launch.

How do you go about delivering it?

The final component is understanding a business's steps to provide and fulfill a single sale. For a startup selling physical goods, this supply chain extends from raw materials through manufacturing, packaging, shipping, delivery, and repeat purchases. For technology companies, this would be your customer journey, from acquisition through onboarding to regular usage and adoption.

If you couldn't answer one or more of those questions, bookmark this section and figure out some reasonably intelligent answers. Once you've written that down, pick things back up here.

---

1. https://www.globenewswire.com/en/news-release/2022/10/28/2543637/0/en/Legal-Tech-Market-to-Achieve-a-Valuation-of-USD-8-2-Billion-by-2029-Witnessing-a-CAGR-of-4-3-Over-the-Forecast-Period-Report-by-Adroit-Market-Research.html

2. https://www.businessofapps.com/data/food-delivery-app-market/
3. https://www.researchandmarkets.com/reports/5302104/pet-toys-global-strategic-business-report

PITCH VERSION CONTROL

Version control. Riveting, I know. But, I promise I'll make this quick. You're going to be making updates to your pitch deck. Making changes to your pitch deck is most likely why you bought this book in the first place!

No pitch deck is ever really truly perfect. You'll be adding slides, removing slides, re-ordering slides, updating slide content, and more usually right up until the last minute before a meeting! Having proper version control is super important to stay organized.

FOR POWERPOINT OR KEYNOTE USERS

If you use Google Slides or an online presentation tool, skip this section.

Naming Your Pitch Deck Files

A lot of times, founders will name their pitch deck versions by the date of their creation. Here are two examples:

Pitch Deck - 01-21-2022.pptx

Deck FINAL - 012122.pptx

I don't recommend this for two reasons. First, the date the file was last updated can be seen from the operating system itself usually by right-clicking the file and selecting "Get Info" or something similar, so putting the date in the file name is a waste of space. Second, many updates will be made in a single day, making including the date in the file name irrelevant.

I also don't recommend including words like "draft" or "final" in the file names. This sort of binary outlook on a pitch deck isn't flexible enough. Like how businesses are constantly testing and learning with their product and optimizing it, founders should look at pitch decks similarly. That's why it's best to think of pitch decks as always being *in beta*. If something is always in beta, it's neither a draft nor a final version. It's simply *the latest version*, like a piece of software. Because of these issues, I recommend using a version number at the end of the filename.

Here're two more examples:

Rhombus Pitch - v3.pptx

Rhombus Pitch - v4.3.pptx

Every time you make a significant update, you would update the version number on the new version. If you'd like to keep it simple, include a round number as the version number (e.g., v1, v2, v3, etc.). At STORY, this is what we do. If you'd like to get a bit more granular with it, you can use a decimal to classify more minor changes (e.g., v1.0, v1.1, v1.2, etc.) and use the first number to classify more considerable changes (e.g., v1.0, v2.0, v3.0, etc.)

Don't Overwrite Past Versions

Whenever you're about to make substantial changes to your deck, duplicate the file and update the version number.

For example:

Rhombus Pitch - v3.pptx
(your latest version)

Rhombus Pitch - v4.pptx
(duplicated version of v3)

After you have completed the above, v4 would be the latest version where we would do all of our work in for that work session. Now, let's say we worked on v4 for three hours, then went away and did something else for several hours, then returned to work on the pitch deck again. Here, I would recommend duplicating v4 and updating the version number again to v5.

Having this level of discipline with your version control and version naming will help keep your life more organized while enabling you to go back in time to explore older versions if needed.

FOR GOOGLE SLIDES OR ONLINE-BASED APPS

If you use Google Slides or any web-based presentation tool or program, you don't need to worry about anything in the previous two sections. Version control is built directly into Google Slides and every other modern presentation tool you can access through a web browser.

In Google Slides, you can see previous versions of your document by clicking on File » Version History » See Version History. This option will open a window with a detailed list of every change ever made to your entire document and who made them. This feature is handy if several team members work on the same presentation.

See, I told you that would be quick! Now, let's jump into improving your pitch deck.

ASSESSING YOUR PITCH

It's time to answer that nagging question posed in the title of this book: *how good is your pitch deck?* The answer is probably "not as good as it can be."

To get more specific (like a lot more specific), I'm going to introduce a scoring system that I call a *lift score*. A lift score is a combination of two other scores: *boosters* and *draggers*. Boosters give investors reasons to believe that your business will succeed. The more boosters you have, the stronger your pitch deck is. Draggers are the opposite, and they contribute to investors thinking that your business won't succeed.

We'll tally up your boosters and draggers and then bring them together to get a quantitative look at how strong your pitch deck is and what's contributing to its strength or lack thereof.

I have one note on this book's points and scoring system. These are my creation, and the point values I assigned are my best guesstimate of the relative importance of each. Some investors would probably disagree with how I distributed my points, while others would likely support it. Investors are all different, and each has its own values and approaches to evaluating businesses as potential investments. Part of the reason why this book exists, to begin with, is that there is no standardized way to pitch a business to investors.

Regardless, the points I allocated to each booster and dragger are still a good rough indicator of a startup's potential strengths and weaknesses. In short, these scoring systems are way better than making blind assumptions, but they're not perfect.

TASTYDRONE
OUR BOOK-LONG EXAMPLE

For the remaining duration of this book, I'll be using a hypothetical startup called TastyDrone in almost every example. TastyDrone is a fictitious company I created for this book. I also use it in my online courses at STORYPitchDecks.com.

This fake startup is a B2C app that uses a fleet of autonomous drones to deliver local restaurant takeout orders to your door. It is a direct competitor with DoorDash, GrubHub, and Uber Eats.

-PART ONE-

EVALUATE YOUR STORY

CHAPTER 1
YOUR STARTUP'S BOOSTERS

BOOSTERS HELP ANSWER THIS QUESTION: *"Why should I, as an investor, believe you can pull this off?"* You can use this list to determine which parts of their business they should focus on improving while at the same time understanding which factors of their business are contributing positively to the overall perception of their startup.

Here is the list of boosters and points associated with each that we'll be looking at in more detail:

Top-notch Team (+3) Highly qualified and accomplished team members in this specific area

Organic Growth (+3) With no marketing, the product has taken off and seen explosive growth

Proven Results (+3) Real data from our solution that proves we're tangibly better than others

Notable Investors (+3) Respected investors are already backing us, demonstrating social proof

Notable Clients (+3) Our client roster includes some of the world's most recognizable brands

Robust Fanbase (+2) We've built a raving community of super fans who can't get enough of us

Healthy Revenue (+2) We have generated a ton of revenue (+1 bonus point for profitable, strong YoY growth)

Superior Design (+2) Wildly superior product design or user experience that eclipses all others

100% Proprietary (+2) What we've created is patent-protected or proprietary and can't be copied

Notable Press (+1) Some of the world's top publications have written about us favorably

Notable Awards (+1) We've received one or many industry awards for our product and company

Unfair Advantage (+1) Our team has insider access, a massive head start, or a pre-built network

Growth Engine (+1) The act of using the product itself incentivizes exponential organic growth

The points listed for each booster are all or nothing. This means that if your startup fits the description, it earns all of the points. If it doesn't, it doesn't get the points. When going through these, be as objective as possible and hard on your startup. Now is the time. Investors most definitely will be, so don't sugarcoat anything.

TIER ONE BOOSTERS

These are the most powerful attributes that can positively impact a startup. They are hard-hitting and very tangible. Tier one boosters are worth three points each.

Top-notch Team (+3 Points)

First thing first for early-stage startups; it's usually all about the strength of the founding members. A top-notch team earning all three points would have at least a decade or more of experience per founding team member in an industry or role specific to the start-up's needs.

For instance, with TastyDrone, investors expect the founding team members to have professional drone experience. Second, investors would also expect TastyDrone founders to have experience with restaurant delivery of some kind, ideally working at a competitor like DoorDash.

Additionally, investors love it when founders have prior experience running a startup. This trait is especially true if a founder has raised capital or successfully exited a past venture. Third, investors would also expect there to be some sort of marketing expert with success in launching and growing a consumer-focused app or marketplace.

Investors look to advisors and board members to fill the gaps if a core founding team lacks skills. For instance, if the founding members of TastyDrone lacked experience with restaurant delivery applications, an advisor or board member with deep expertise in this area would satisfy these essential criteria for investors.

On the other hand, if a founding team has only a few years of experience in an irrelevant industry, they wouldn't earn points here.

Organic Growth (+3 Points)

Growth is good, but organic growth is better. Good organic growth is usually a good sign that a product or service is so fantastic that people talk about it and recommend it to others. Usually, this means that if founders threw marketing dollars or formalized sales efforts at the startup, it would yield immediately noticeable and outsized results. If you need a number, I'd say good organic growth would be anything over 15% or 20% on an annual or monthly basis with multiple months or years at that same rate.

Using our TastyDrone example, let's assume they decided to launch in Austin, TX, and they previously contacted ten restaurants to participate in a pilot program. If any signed up, that is not organic growth. But, if 20 more restaurants reached out to TastyDrone over the coming weeks and expressed their strong interest in being a part of the program because they heard about the company from a friend or fellow restaurant owner, this would be considered organic growth. The same principle applies to online organic growth as well.

Proven Results (+3 Points)

Proven results mean the startup has tangible, concrete evidence or data that their solution is better than their competitors or alternatives. For instance, if a company can say, "we are ten times faster versus the category leaders," or "we double team productivity for half the cost of doing it on your own," these are clear and tangible results that prove a startup's solution is superior.

Typically, founders can obtain these sorts with a tiny bit of research. For instance, if a company has a couple of initial clients or early pilot programs, it could be as simple as surveying existing users or customers to get their opinions on a startup's offering. This data is probably the most powerful thing for an early-stage company to obtain, yet it's one of the things we see the least among startup founders.

To go back to our TastyDrone example, we could aim to say that our drones deliver food to restaurant customers 50% faster than human drivers. This data point on speed can be obtained through a pilot program with a partner restaurant and measured throughout a few dozen deliveries or more. In addition to speed, we could also say that our fee structure for restaurants is half as expensive compared to companies like DoorDash or Uber Eats. One of the founders of TastyDrone could simply approach restaurants in the area and ask them to participate in a pilot for no charge.

As long as the founders collect data at every turn and multiple tests are run, the startup will not only have data from one delivery but potentially dozens of deliveries. In addition, the founders can also order food from that restaurant using DoorDash or Uber Eats to the exact locations that their drones delivered to. This method would allow the founders to compare their drones' speed to human drivers. Now, does it take a bit of work to gather this data? Yes. Does it also go a long way in showcasing the potential power of TastyDrones's solution versus the current alternatives? Absolutely.

As for the cost data, the founders could gather this during the delivery speed pilot program by noting the fees charged to all parties. In this case, it would be a TastyDrone founder ordering delivery using an app like DoorDash. Let's assume DoorDash charges an average fee of $10 to the customer and $5 to the restaurant.

Since TastyDrone can set its prices to whatever they want, it could aim for 50% lower fees than DoorDash. Being able to say this would look great in a pitch deck and an advertising campaign to attract customers. To achieve this, TastyDrone could implement a $5 flat fee to the customer and another $2.50 flat fee to the restaurant. With these price points, TastyDrone could now officially claim it's 50% more affordable than the category leader. One final note here, it's only sometimes better to cost less than your competitors. Most of the time, investors won't want to see startups competing exclusively on price. If this were the case, investors would view this as leaving money on the table that could spark a price war, which isn't good for anyone. However, with TastyDrone, we're assuming that a fundamental problem within the category is the outrageously high fees charged to restaurants and customers.

. . .

Notable Investors (+3 Points)

Many investors avoid being the first to invest in a company. There's considerable risk for ultra-early-stage investments. Success is anything but guaranteed. But, as soon as a startup secures its first investor, it becomes much easier to land additional capital. Prospective investors now see the startup as lower risk. They think, "If investor A invested, I should consider this opportunity before dismissing it." At STORY, we usually put investor logos on our pitch deck's title slide to show it off from the beginning. Just be sure to get permission first.

Founders who have yet to raise investor capital do not qualify for this booster.

Notable Clients (+3 Points)

This is specific to B2B companies. Similar to notable investors, notable clients or customer brands go a long way in demonstrating promise.

As a good rule, anyone on the Fortune 1000 list could be considered a notable client. I also think of industry leaders as notable clients even if they weren't on the Fortune 1000.

As for TastyDrone, this could apply if a notable restaurant chain signed up to be a customer. For instance, if a Chipotle location were a pilot or trial current customer, the business would qualify for the three points awarded for notable clients because it's a $45 billion company with global reach. However, if TastyDrone's only customers were a tiny, local deli, they would not qualify for these three points. Simply having a paying client or customer doesn't mean they're notable.

————

TIER TWO BOOSTERS

The next level of boosters is still significant but doesn't necessarily yield the same weight as the first tier. Even better, a few of these items are relatively easy to implement if a startup lacks tier-one boosters.

Robust Fanbase (+2 Points)

A fan base helps advocate for the company to others unfamiliar. This specific booster doesn't necessarily apply to all startups. However, startups that have managed to amass a community of loyal supporters have an asset in the eyes of investors. Moreover, investors take this as a sign that the startup is close to achieving product-market fit, as people are willing to pay for the solution and go onto forums and social media to spread the good word about it.

Communities of fans are widespread among physical products and software sold to individual consumers. Companies that sell B2B could also have robust fan bases built from the employees or individuals within the business using the startup's product.

For our TastyDrone example, the pilot or early trial customers ordering from restaurants could be an excellent source to create a fan base.

The best way to showcase a fan base within your pitch deck is by including short user or customer quotes and testimonials. Reviews and ratings on sites like G2.com, trustpilot.com, or an app store are perfect for including here.

In terms of fanbase size, "good" is very startup-dependent. Is a hundred fans a lot? A hundred could be a lot for a pre-launch company with no marketing budget. Or, for a Series-A B2B company, a hundred raving enterprises could be a massive fan base. But, for a company that's been around for ten years, a hundred fans is tiny. If you feel you've got a solid community of fans around your startup, you probably qualify for the points here.

No fans? No points. Sorry.

Healthy Revenue (+2 Points)

This applies to companies earning revenue. "Healthy" is a subjective term, but in my experience, anything between $250k and $1 million in revenue in the first year or two of operations is relatively healthy. Why is it important to talk about revenue? Revenue is the number one thing that will increase a company's valuation. Analysts usually peg the company's valuation to revenue, and higher valuations lead to higher investor returns.

TastyDrone is pre-revenue, so showing healthy revenue isn't possible. However, the next best thing for pre-revenue companies to show instead of healthy revenue is what is known as LOIs, or letters of intent. A letter of intent is a formal statement from a prospective customer that says they will purchase your product or services upon launch.

While a few LOIs from notable companies help, they're not the same as having actual revenue from those clients. But, if your startup has multiple LOIs but no revenue, call this one point instead of two points.

Nada revenue? Nada points.

Superior Design (+2 Points)

Good design conveys trust. Some people even say that good design is a *business requirement*. The good news is that this is one attribute a founder can control from the first day they start working on their startup.

Of note, design doesn't just mean the design of your pitch deck. Design touches every visual element of your business. It includes your logo, product, website, social media presence, and more.

Apple has built one of the most valuable brands in the world using design as a core tenant of the business's success. Starbucks and Nike aren't far behind. I come from a branding background and put a ton of weight on how well a brand communicates visually. It also looks bizarre if the pitch deck design is impressive but the product is subpar. The same thing applies if flipped around. If a company has great product design or user experience, but terrible pitch deck design, there's a misalignment of the brand's visual communication.

Nowadays, good design is relatively accessible, and founders don't have an excuse to ignore it. Freelancers and online tools

If you're the founder of a startup and you're not sure if your design is top-notch, head to a freelancer website like Upwork.com or Fiverr.com and enlist the help of a professional. If you're on a budget, head to a website like 99designs.com. Here, you pay a flat fee, and designers worldwide compete against each other to create the best design.

Once a founder has the basis for their brand design, it's crucial to ensure that the product's design brings that brand to life. If it's software, this means emphasizing user experience in front-end web design. If it's a physical product, that means enlisting the help of a seasoned industrial designer to create something that people will love to use.

For TastyDrone, we have created a couple of mock-ups with TastyDrone logo on the drones and take-out box payloads. We even made a fictitious phone app mockup with the same branding. This visual consistency across mediums and channels plays into how well a brand articulates itself through the language of design.

Good design is so powerful that it can cover up blatant strategic weaknesses that investors would otherwise call out. But don't think that you should just pay a boatload for a great pitch deck designer and ignore the content. Investors will see right through that.

You don't earn points here if your brand or product looks older than five years from whenever you read this.

100% Proprietary (+2 Points)

Investors want to see something unique. The last tier two booster is proprietary technology, which could include a proprietary process.

The apex of proprietary technology is securing a formal patent. However, there are a few legal nuances that come with patents. A filed patent is good but doesn't offer legal protection yet. But when the USPTO grants a patent, complete legal protection is in place, providing a tremendous competitive advantage. It's an ideal scenario for investors if the solution is also excellent and patented. Investors want to believe that whatever you've created is challenging (or illegal) to copy or replicate.

What's to stop a massive company like Google from making a similar product? A patent, that's what.

What if you don't have any patents filed or granted? In the case of TastyDrone, we're assuming the company doesn't have any patents that are filed or granted. However, this fictitious company has invested heavily in creating two elements that are 100% proprietary and created in-house: an autonomous, AI-based drone piloting system and a physical drone docking station. These two elements dig a significant competitive moat around the business. New or existing companies that wish to compete with TastyDrone must also create similar technology.

Since this is the case, TastyDrone would receive both points for this booster.

———

TIER THREE BOOSTERS

Boosters in this tier are worth only one point, but they're still important. I've got more good news here for founders: earning points for these boosters is pretty straightforward and doesn't require much effort.

. . .

Notable Press (+1 Point)

Getting mentioned in the press is somewhat easy. Usually, all it takes is enlisting the help of a public relations (PR) firm or freelancer. Services typically start at a couple thousand dollars a month, and contracts can last a few months to a year.

For companies just starting out with PR, it's common for initial press pickups to be from smaller publications. As smaller publications cover the company, your PR professional will use these as proof points to pitch your business to better-known publications. Within three to six months, a startup can get coverage from major press publications like the Wall Street Journal, Forbes, TechCrunch, and more.

Press mentions are usually a good indicator that whatever the business is up to is newsworthy and might be worth an investor's attention. However, since good press is something that can be bought and not necessarily earned organically, we've only allocated one point to this booster.

In the case of TastyDrone, we might assume that a local newspaper or blog has covered what the startup is up to. Local news networks, local papers, local blogs, and local podcasts in the Austin area (where our fictitious company is based) are all excellent potential places to start.

Notable Awards (+1 Point)

Similar to press, industry awards and startup awards are good indicators for investors to pay closer attention to a startup. However, sometimes winning an award isn't as complicated as it may seem. Usually, all it takes is a little bit of research to pinpoint potential awards, then more research to define the winning criteria for those awards, and then writing it all up in a submission and submitting it.

Also of note, accelerators could fall under notable awards. Getting into an accelerator can be a good indicator for an investor to pay attention. However, just because an accelerator accepted your startup and you participated, it doesn't guarantee you will land investor capital. Accelerators help prepare a startup for growth and investment, but not all startups need accelerators. We've got some good research on whether or not startups should join an accelerator on our website.

For TastyDrone, the founders could consider local technology, restaurant innovation, or startup awards. We recommend featuring notable awards or accelerators on the title and traction slides.

Unfair Advantage (+1 Point)

An unfair advantage can mean many things. I define this as some sort of significant leg up on the competition. For example, this could be a founder's extensive industry network that helps lock in initial customers. Another unfair advantage could be insider access to high-value data that is usually hard to obtain. One more example could be a formal partnership that accelerates early-stage growth.

Alternatively, founders could have an unfair advantage by bringing high-value skills, like performance digital marketing. This particular skill is high value because it would mean the startup could drive new user acquisition for a lower cost than its competitors.

For TastyDrone, this unfair advantage could be that a founding team member is a leading expert on coding autonomous drone piloting software. Talk about an unfair advantage! Or, TastyDrone could form a strategic partnership with one of the top drone manufacturers in China.

If you can't identify your unfair advantage, start by making a list. Write down an unfair advantage wish list. On this list is everything a startup in your category could wish for that would make you the strongest competitor. Next, go down the list and see which ones are the easiest to obtain, and then go out and get them. It could be as simple as reaching out to an excellent potential advisor or as easy as starting conversations with a prospective strategic partner who could provide an advantage down the road.

Growth Engine (+1 Point)

A growth engine is a business strategy that incentivizes users to share or invite new users. For instance, a startup that focuses on creating tools for influencers could offer incentives for its users to share their product on social in exchange for a cut of any new user revenue. I don't hear or see industry experts talk about growth engines much, but I have seen plenty of examples with the startups I've worked with.

In the case of TastyDrone, it could be an incentive program for customers to send an invite link to their friends to get their first TastyDrone order for free, while the original user would get their next order for free if their friend signs up. Usually, affiliate and influencer programs would fall under this bucket as long as the founders have embedded those programs into the startup's solution. Founders should look for ways to utilize their existing customers to grow their user base without the business taking on additional upfront costs.

———

Now that we've covered the boosters that can provide credibility to a startup, we'll look at draggers next.

CHAPTER 2
YOUR STARTUP'S DRAGGERS

DRAGGERS ARE things that detract from how investors view your startup. These attributes tend to make your startup look bad. Unlike boosters, draggers are reasons *not* to believe and usually instill doubt in an investor's mind.

To remix a quote from Frank Herbert's sci-fi classic *Dune*, *"I must not instill doubt. Doubt is the deal-killer."*

Here's the list of draggers:

Negative Press (-3) Unfortunately, our company has been in the cross-fire of some bad PR

Shaky Markets (-3) Our sector has gotten a bad wrap lately because of negative market news

Negative Reviews (-3) Customers haven't been too happy with us, and they have let others know

Product Parity (-2) Our product isn't that different from what's already out there

Slow Momentum (-2) It's taken years to get to this point, and we're still not where we want to be

Rookie Founders (-2) Our founders are green and don't have much experience in this area at all

Untested Product (-2) We're pre-launch or post-launch and don't have any data or results yet

Outdated Design (-2) If we're being honest, the design and experience of our product seem old

No Competitors (-2) We don't have any competitors because we're so unique and different

Leadership Gaps (-1) To succeed, we will need to have X person, and we don't have them yet

Unfound Founders (-1) We don't really do LinkedIn, and you can't find anything about us online

———

TIER ONE DRAGGERS

The first tier of draggers affect a startup in the most negative way possible. Unfortunately, these attributes are sometimes out of the founder's control. If any of these are bad enough, it could be an instant deal killer for some investors.

. . .

Negative Press (-3 Points)

Negative press isn't something a company would try to earn on purpose. Negative press usually results from a company making a mistake. Unfavorable PR could originate from poor business performance, a social media slip-up, shady business practices, or taking advantage of a marginalized population. In the odd case that negative press is simply inaccurate, founders should have a direct and honest conversation with investors if asked about it.

Regardless, sometimes the only way to fix negative press is to improve whatever attracted it in the first place. Either way, the saying "any PR is good PR" isn't true in the startup world. If a company is getting slammed by inaccurate information in the press, there's still probably a small kernel of truth buried in it.

In short, avoid negative press by avoiding poor business practices that would attract it in the first place.

Shaky Markets (-3 Points)

When overall economic market conditions are poor, or a particular sector faces scrutiny, investors get scared. However, these things are usually out of your control as a founder.

There could be a few factors contributing to shaky markets. The first is how current category leaders are performing. For instance, in 2022, Beyond Meat had a rough year. Once the darling of the plant-based protein industry, their stock lost nearly 80% of its value that year, and they laid off 200 employees in Q4 2022. When investors see a leader falter, they can often take this as an indicator that the plant-based alternative proteins space might be cooling off. As a result, startups in this industry might have a rough time raising funds, especially if they are a direct competitor to Beyond Meat and need more differentiation in their business model.

Another factor that could play into shaky markets is unstable supply chains. If certain raw materials are hard to buy or are over-priced, it directly affects the companies downstream and their ability to maintain profitable operations.

In the case of TastyDrone, because this fictitious company manu-factures most of its drones and docking stations in China, supply chain disruptions could severely limit the company's growth potential. What would they do if they needed to order 10,000 drones ASAP but couldn't import them because of an unexpected embargo or pandemic?

The key takeaway here for founders is to do their homework. Read your industry extensively and see what experts say about it. Then, consider how investors might look at that information as they consider your company.

Negative Reviews (-3 Points)

Similar to negative press, it's likely that customers aren't happy if a company's online reviews are negative (e.g., one or two stars out of five). Companies with negative reviews are most likely not listening to their customers, and those that don't listen to their customers don't stay in business for long. Investors do their research; all it takes is a simple Google search for your startup's name to see how current customers are discussing it. Forums, Reddit posts, Google reviews, G2.com, and ProductHunt.com are all sites that appear on the first page of search results that provide heightened visibility to investors.

If TastyDrone customers were leaving online reviews about how their food was damaged or destroyed in transit by a drone, this is a big deal. If the food doesn't get there safely, it defeats the entire purpose of the business. If the TastyDrone founders needed to build a pitch deck, and this was the case, I might recommend including a slide that directly addresses the fact that they're aware of it and are actively trying to fix the problem.

You can't please everyone, and negative reviews happen. They're a part of doing business today. As long as you are taking action, measurable, and impactful steps to address bad reviews, that could be enough for investors to see that you're doing your best to improve.

———

TIER TWO DRAGGERS

With some foresight, founders can avoid this next tier of draggers. I'd like to urge founders to look through this list and find ways to fix some of these today. Sometimes all it takes is an afternoon of work, and founders can eliminate one or more of these draggers from their startup's story.

Product Parity (-2 Points)

Copycat products are underwhelming. Businesses that saw an opportunity and decided to jump on the bandwagon by doing the same thing as everyone else in the category are boring to investors.

Is it possible to build a multi-billion dollar business this way? Yes. Just look at Pepsi. If your startup's product or service is essentially just a copy of an existing offering, it's unlikely that an investor will see something special in it. Banks might if you wanted them to give you a loan, but probably not venture capital or startup investors.

An easy way to avoid this is to have at least one major differentiator. Here are a few examples: superior users experience, superior product design, a better sales process, or a piece of in-house tech that makes you more efficient. In just a bit, I will introduce you to a concept to help you decide *what type* of differentiator will be best for your startup. But for now, identifying one small but critical difference in your feature set can be enough to satisfy investors that you've got a competitive advantage.

A social cause factored into your operations could help your startup stand out. Tom's Shoes is a good example. They donate one pair of shoes for every pair sold.

TastyDrone's business fundamentally differs from existing category leaders because they use drones to deliver payloads instead of human drivers. Therefore, TastyDrone wouldn't be at product parity and wouldn't receive the negative points here.

Slow Momentum (-2 Points)

We never like to see slow momentum when working on a pitch deck. What I mean by slow momentum is when a company looks like they're moving at a slow pace.

Here's an example. Imagine a company that raised $2M in Seed funding in 2016. Imagine it's now 2023, and the company is still working on developing its product. Pharmaceutical or deep tech companies might be okay with ten-year time horizons as research can take time. But most startups fall outside of these exceptions, and slow momentum usually indicates to investors that the founders might lack the ability to get things done.

Of the clients we've worked with, the ones who have raised the most often are companies founded, developed, and launched within a year or two on a minimal budget.

Most investors believe that the best way to see if a business has potential is not to wait for everything to be perfect to launch. Instead, they prefer companies launch faster with a minimum viable product (MVP) that can be tested in-market sooner and optimized later. Startups can hasten timelines to find product-market fit this way. For startups, perfection is the enemy of productivity.

For TastyDrone, this fake business took a year to create the drone piloting software. At the same time, the company was developing its proprietary docking stations in partnership with a manufacturer in China. Taking a year or more to make innovative and valuable technology that didn't exist before is usually seen as a good thing. But, if TastyDrone had spent the last seven years trying to get things right and still didn't have a single pilot test, it's probably a case of slow momentum, and this would reflect poorly on the company's founders.

Rookie Founders (-2 Points)

Mainstream media might lead you to believe that only the 20-something geniuses are winning the startup CEO game. But, in 2020, MIT, Wharton, and Northwest University conducted a study in partnership with the US Census Bureau called *Age and High-Growth Entrepreneurship*. The study found that the older a founder was, the greater their chances of success. For instance, a 50-year-old is twice as likely to start a company that leads to a successful exit as a 30-year-old. The experience that comes along with age is precious.

If you and your co-founders just graduated college and lack professional experience, your chances of raising are not impossible, just slim. While it's true that 20-year-olds and inexperienced founders don't have all the baggage and biases of their older counterparts and are tackling older problems in wildly innovative ways, a lack of actual business experience hurts the optics of your startup.

I highly encourage founders with little or no experience to create a fantastic board of advisors and hire experienced leaders to help them build the future together, which kills two birds with one stone. It ensures that the startup has the best type of experience in place, and it masks the founder's lack of experience at the same time.

We once worked with a founder who operated within the AI video generation space. His background was in marketing, and he lacked technical, operational, and financial expertise. Not ideal for a CEO. So, he researched who the top experts were in his hyper-niche industry. Next, he contacted each of them and recruited them for his leadership team and advisory board. The team included Ph.D. candidates from top universities and even former leadership from a competitor. Because the rest of the team was so strong, the founder's lack of experience became less of an issue in investor meetings.

With TastyDrone, we imagined an ideal scenario and assumed that the founding team members all have at least 10-15 years of relevant industry experience, including past employment at Fortune 1000 companies.

Untested Product (-2 Points)

When a company develops something and doesn't customer conduct research to see if people are willing to pay for it or not, it's an untested product. An untested product or solution is a risk to investors because they have no indicator of whether or not people are willing to pay for it.

Beta and pilot programs are usually the best way for founders to avoid this dragger. It's also something that founders should be doing in general because it de-risks the business for the founder. By opening up a product to potential customers earlier in its development, founders can quickly identify and correct product flaws before they hit the market instead of wasting years working on an incorrect assumption. By testing early, founders can also receive valuable feedback that they can use to improve their marketing, sales, and communication efforts.

In the case of TastyDrone, we assumed that the business had conducted at least one or two pilot programs with local restaurants in their area. In these programs, the founders carefully monitored and recorded every data point from each delivery. We also assume that the founders interviewed the restaurants to understand their experience with TastyDrone. Investors would love to hear this as it means the team can listen, learn, and react to market signals.

To sum up, test your product and improve based on those tests. Taking these steps will improve your chances of success at the business level, and including these activities in your pitch deck will undoubtedly boost your optics.

Outdated Design (-2 Points)

This one can be a little subjective, but I will shed some light on it. Design is constantly changing, and there is such a thing as modern design and outdated design. What's modern now will be obsolete in 20 years, sometimes much faster.

As a quick exercise, head to Google and do an image search for "Uber app interface 2011." After reviewing a few of the results, do another search for "Uber app interface 2023" (or whatever year you're reading this) and compare that to what it looked like in 2011. The app's latest and greatest iteration looks much better. It's clean, simple, intuitive, and powerful.

Design language is constantly changing, just like spoken language. If founders decide to cut corners by pinching pennies on design, they will end up with a cheap design. Things that look cheap look untrustworthy, which is the opposite of what we're trying to do with a pitch deck.

As I said in the booster section about design, the easiest way to avoid this is to enlist the help of a credible, experienced designer. The term "you get what you pay for" applies here.

That said, should a startup without revenue pay $25,000 for a logo? Probably not. But, two years later, if that same startup were on track to earn $5 million in revenue with a healthy margin, it would probably be time to invest in that $25,000 rebrand.

In 2014, the Design Management Institute conducted a study of 75 Fortune 500 companies that emphasized design more than other companies of similar size. They found that the companies that emphasized design (like Apple) outperformed the S&P 500 by 228%. As I said previously, good design is a business requirement.

Let's say TastyDrone created the first version of their deck in mid-2021. At the time, their design and branding were somewhat modern. But, looking at it again in 2023, I know we can do better. So, while we're overhauling the story and content from top to bottom using the techniques in this book, we're also going to upgrade the look and feel.

No Competition (-2 Points)

Every business should have competitors or current alternatives. Competitors fall into three buckets. Let's use TastyDrone to address each one:

1. Direct Competitors
2. Indirect Competitors
3. Current Alternatives

Direct competitors would be other drone delivery services, and when I wrote the first version of the TastyDrone deck in 2021, there weren't any around. Now in 2023, there are a few that have popped up. If I were TastyDrone's founder, I would *love* to see that because it means that other people believed that there was enough opportunity in the drone delivery space to start a business. It would be even better if they landed some funding because I would bring that up in my pitch in a way that would show potential investors that this market was heating up and showing promise.

Direct competitors would also include DoorDash, GrubHub, and Uber Eats. If we were lying to ourselves, we could group these category leaders into an indirect competitor category. I think that would be a mistake because these businesses compete for the same dollar from the same target.

In-house delivery drivers could be considered indirect competitors. For example, most pizza places have a couple of delivery drivers on staff.

We could categorize those who opt to pick up the food themselves as current alternatives. Because recipe boxes like Hello Fresh address the same problem for the same audience, we could consider them a current alternative. Their audiences are both saying, "I'm hungry and don't want to leave my home," in different ways.

Startup founders must understand the competitive and current alternatives landscape before talking to any investor. Again, if a founder claims that their startup has competition, investors will likely perceive this negatively. A lack of competition usually means that no market is established or available to capture. It also comes across to investors like the founder, who refused to do their homework or turned a blind eye to very real competitive threats.

———

TIER THREE DRAGGERS

Founders can fix the draggers in this tier with some homework. There are only two attributes:

. . .

Leadership Gaps (-1 Point)

We conducted an in-depth study of the top questions investors are most likely to ask during a pitch meeting. Investors are most likely to ask questions about the founding team. To get more specific, the most common question we encountered was, *"What gaps currently exist in your team?"*

Investors want to see that founders know about their skill gaps and are taking action to fill them with top-notch talent.

Again, let's use our TastyDrone example. Even before looking at the team slide, we can create a picture of what the ideal team should look like. First, the company most likely needs some sort of developer with expertise in autonomous vehicle piloting software. Next, since hardware manufacturing is involved, the company probably needs someone with that experience. That's two roles so far. After that, the company would also need someone with experience in leading operations at a company with high logistical complexity. Then, we could also look for someone to help with finance and someone to lead marketing and sales. We're looking at five roles that ideally need to be addressed by individuals on the leadership team or advisory board.

Knowing who you need is the first place to start. Next, founders can search for advisors, part-time co-founders, and fractional CXOs to help fill the gaps. If you are actively hiring, an easy way to call this out in your pitch deck is by including a "coming soon" section on your team slide that identifies your open hire roles.

Unfound Founders (-1 Point)

Odds are, investors will do an online search for you and your founding team members, expecting to find you. They hope to see a LinkedIn page at minimum to verify that you're a real person with real experience.

Founders should ensure they have *something* online that investors can find, and a LinkedIn profile is straightforward to create or update. At the bare minimum, your LinkedIn profile should have a professional-looking headshot and a complete resume of your experience and education.

Lastly, use your real name. For some reason, we noticed a trend with Web3 founders using their Discord names instead of their birth names (Discord is an online chat room application). Don't do that. No one's going to invest in your crypto startup, DaRealDuckyBoi247.

———

Between our lists of boosters and draggers, you can now comprehensively assess your startup's perceived strengths and weaknesses. In our next section, we will combine these two things in what I call a *lift score*.

CHAPTER 3
YOUR LIFT SCORE

OKAY, so you've tallied up your boosters and draggers...now what?

Now we combine your scores and look at each side by side. The result of this comparison is what I call a lift score, and it provides a quantitative look at the overall strength of your pitch.

We'll use TastyDrone as our example score:

TastyDrone Booster Score: +13

Top-notch Team (+3) Highly qualified and accomplished team members in this specific area

Proven Results (+3) Real data from our solution that proves we're tangibly better than others

Notable Clients (+3) Our client roster includes some of the world's most recognizable brands

100% Proprietary (+2) What we've created is patent-protected or proprietary and can't be copied

Notable Awards (+1) We've received one or many industry awards for our product and company

Growth Engine (+1) The act of using the product itself incentivizes exponential organic growth

TastyDrone Dragger Score: -4

Shaky Markets (-3) Our sector has gotten a bad wrap lately because of negative market news

Leadership Gaps (-1) To succeed, we will need to have X person, and we don't have them, yet

We can calculate the lift score by subtracting your dragger score from your booster score.

TastyDrone Lift Score: +9

- Booster score: +13
- Dragger score: -4
- Lift score: (13 - 4) = +9

EVALUATING YOUR LIFT SCORE

Before you immediately want to know how your score compares to others, slow it down first. These scores don't work that way. It's almost irrelevant to know how your score compares to others because this scoring system is all about knowing *your* strengths and weaknesses in presenting *your* business.

So, instead of getting all competitive with others, get competitive with yourself. The booster-dragger-life scoring framework is for knowing where your strengths and weaknesses are so you can take active steps to mitigate or emphasize those in your pitch deck.

Let's look at the TastyDrone score again:

Booster score: +13
Top-notch Team, Proven Results, Notable Clients, 100% Proprietary, Notable Awards, Growth Engine

Dragger score: -4
Shaky Markets, Leadership Gaps

Lift score: +9

The person preparing the TastyDrone pitch deck would make sure that each of the boosters they scored points for was called out and highlighted in the pitch deck. Don't bury your boosters in an appendix or make it a voice-over-only part of your pitch. Some may deserve their own slide, and others may be a sentence or bullet point. These elements are the things that investors will care about, so founders must make sure they're prevalent in their pitch.

Next, we'll refer back to our master booster list to see if there's anything else we could include to provide additional credibility. Look for boosters you nearly qualified for but didn't because of a tiny issue. Nows your chance to try and fix those issues, so the version of your pitch is much more powerful.

If you're a B2B startup that's pre-revenue, one idea might be to go out and get letters of intent (LOIs) from big brands. Looking at TastyDrone (who is also somewhat B2B and pre-revenue), they could approach the corporate headquarters of a few notable restaurant chains, pitch them on TastyDrone, and ask for an LOI at the end of the meeting. Imagine saying, "Besides our successful pilot programs, we have signed LOIs from Taco Bell, Pizza Hut, and Starbucks." Talk about a hell of a slide! And all it cost the owners was a hefty helping of persistence and some emails.

Another idea for TastyDrone would be to dial up the power of its existing strengths, like our 100% proprietary technology. If you recall, the business hadn't filed patents even though they had developed their hardware and software in-house. The founders could spend a few hundred bucks enlisting the help of a patent attorney to file for the protection of their piloting software and docking stations. Then, at the very least, the founders could say that they have formally filed patents for their technology secret sauce.

The next job for TastyDrone would be to see if they can eliminate or mitigate some of those draggers: shaky markets and leadership gaps.

As mentioned, there's not much anyone can do about shaky markets, but the founder could consider addressing it directly in their pitch deck. Suppose they added a slide that mentioned what was happening at the macroeconomic level and how the company was taking steps to mitigate those effects at the microeconomic level. In that case, this could fly well with investors. It would show them that the founders knew the market conditions and had a clear plan to come out on top when things settled down.

The second dragger, leadership gaps, can also be addressed in their pitch deck by including a "coming soon" section on their team slide. In the meantime, the founders could also consider adding advisors to fill those gaps until bringing on full-time staff.

———

There we go! Now that we've made significant strides toward strengthening your startup's story, we will take it to the next level by ensuring it appears ideally positioned to succeed in a given industry. I'll introduce you to a new tool called the *storyline compass*. It is another quantitative tool I created to show founders how they can improve their startup's positioning within their broader industry.

But first, a recap of part one.

PART ONE RECAP
EVALUATE YOUR STORY

1. **Score your boosters** and note each one in your current pitch deck, noting how prevalent each booster is or isn't featured in it.

2. **Score your draggers** and note each one in your current pitch deck, noting how prevalent each dragger is or isn't featured in it.

3. **Calculate your lift score** by subtracting your dragger score from your booster score. Note this down somewhere on your current version of your pitch deck.

4. **Create a new version of your deck** before you begin your edits on the new version.

5. **Dial-up each booster** in your pitch deck, ensuring each one is conspicuous and not buried somewhere in an appendix slide.

6. **Try to add more boosters** by looking back at the master booster list to see if you can earn a few more points; especially look for the boosters you almost earned but didn't because of a minor issue.

7. **Mitigate your draggers** and judge whether or not you should call each out in your pitch deck. Only bring up a dragger if you have a clear plan to fix and be sure to put it on the same slide.

8. **Recalculate your boosters, draggers, and lift score** with the new version of your deck to see where you improved!

-PART TWO-

ELEVATE YOUR STRENGTHS

CHAPTER 4
THE STORYLINE COMPASS

THE FIRST PART of this book was about creating a fast, surface understanding of what founders can do to improve their pitch deck quickly. This section will dive deeper into how the business is positioned relative to its competition.

Our primary tool for this and the book's final section is a *storyline compass*. The storyline compass is a quadrant-based tool with two logical and emotional business vectors.

THE FOUR VECTORS OF THE STORYLINE COMPASS

More Effective (Logical Decision) It does a better job or gets better results.

More Accessible (Logical Decision) It's easier, faster, or cheaper to access.

More Enjoyable (Emotional Decision) It's prettier, or more fun, or simpler.

More Connection (Emotional Decision) It provides more emotional value.

Together, these four vectors represent every possible benefit a company could provide its customers. In part one, boosters and draggers were more of an inward-looking tool where the comparison to competitors wasn't needed. With the storyline compass, however, comparing it with other companies is mandatory to complete it.

To create a storyline compass, founders rank their startup on a scale of one to ten for each of the four vectors. You would then repeat the process for at least two more competitors. Regarding the scoring, one is not at all, and ten is the most amount possible. So, when founders are looking at the More Effective vector, they would rank the effectiveness of their solution to the effectiveness of other competitors in the category addressing the same underlying problem.

This exercise makes sense when we compare each vector across several companies in the same industry to our startup. Only when we do this will it become clear which solution is winning and in what way.

It's important to note that the storyline compass also considers a startup's target audience. For instance, two companies within the same industry will cater to small and medium businesses, while others will cater to larger businesses and enterprises. As a result, these different target audiences will yield different outcomes in the storyline compass.

Let's cover a quick real-world example using TastyDrone. For the restaurant and takeout delivery apps industry, we could define each vector as follows:

1. **Effective** - A logical vector that answers the question, "How correct was the order, and was it transported safely?"
2. **Accessible** - A logical vector that answers the question, "How fast did the order arrive, and how affordable was it?"
3. **Enjoyable** - An emotional vector that answers, "How easy was the end-to-end ordering and delivery experience?"
4. **Connection** - An emotional vector that answers, "How much of an emotional connection did the company create during the experience?"

I'll demonstrate how this works by creating a storyline compass for TastyDrone. Again, the points I'm awarding are subjective on a scale from one to ten. Furthermore, because you're reading this in black-and-white, I have broken out these compasses into two versions to make things easier to visualize. However, when doing this on your own, you can just make each company a different color and use a single radar chart.

EXAMPLE #1: TASTYDRONE VS. DIRECT COMPETITORS

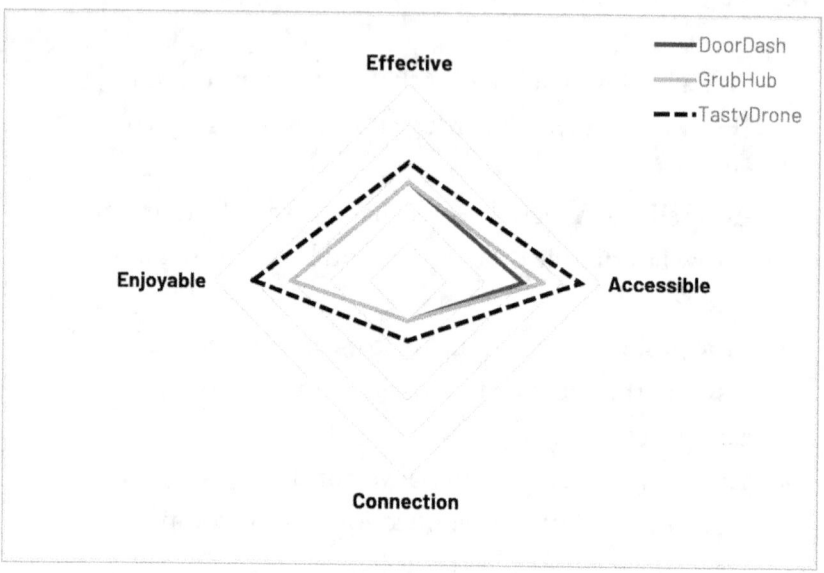

Above, I've compared the benefits of TastyDrone with the benefits of GrubHub and DoorDash. We could also add Uber Eats, but they would be very close to DoorDash and GrubHub. Notice how DoorDash and GrubHub also overlap on nearly all metrics. I found DoorDash's app a little easier to use and gave it a better score in accessibility than GrubHub.

Founders can create a storyline compass in any spreadsheet software like Google Sheets or Excel. To make a storyline compass like this, set up your data table (example below) and select Radar Chart from the chart creation menu in your respective software. You don't need to make it black and white, but I have done so for this book so you can more easily view the data.

I used the data below to create the compass above:

Effective
TastyDrone: 6
DoorDash: 5
GrubHub: 5

Accessible
TastyDrone: 9
DoorDash: 6
GrubHub: 7

Enjoyable
TastyDrone: 8
DoorDash: 6
GrubHub: 6

Connection
TastyDrone: 3
DoorDash: 2
GrubHub: 2

As a reminder, these are all subjective numbers I made up to compare each company across the four vectors.

Here's my thinking for each.

EFFECTIVE

A logical vector that answers the question, "How correct was the order, and was it undamaged?"

Overall, efficacy in this category is at parity across the providers. Every order should be correct, and every order should arrive undamaged. Therefore, there isn't much room for one company to excel over the other.

TastyDrone: 6

Almost every single order arrived correctly and intact. However, TastyDrone could have a slight edge here if the drones flew with more stability than cars.

DoorDash and GrubHub: 5

Practically, every order arrived correctly and nearly every order is intact.

ACCESSIBLE

A logical vector that answers the question, "How fast did the order arrive, and how affordable was it?"

Accessibility is one of the primary vectors that most competitors compete on within this category. As a result, we're going to label this vector as our *linchpin vector*. I'll talk more about linchpin vectors in just a minute, but a linchpin vector is the most essential factor for a given sector and audience. For restaurant delivery apps, people decide on which to use for convenience: fast delivery speeds and low costs. In an ideal world, free food would show up on our plates instantaneously. The companies closest to this vision in the eyes of the market will be the long-term winners.

I found an online data table to help with this comparison (source). Of note, I only used the data for DoorDash and GrubHub.

Applying that information and combining it with TastyDrone's fictional pilot programs, here is the vector scoring and how I got there:

TastyDrone: 9
$18.58 meal price
$5 fee/meal (27%)
15 min delivery time

DoorDash: 6
$18.58 meal price
$12.81 fee (58%)
25 min delivery time

GrubHub: 7
$18.58 meal price
$9.45 fee (41%)
25 min delivery time

TastyDrone has lower fees, and a faster delivery time; therefore, I ranked it higher vs. DoorDash and GrubHub for accessibility.

DoorDash has the; most expensive fees but identical delivery times vs. GrubHub; consequently, I rated it slightly lower.

GrubHub has slightly; lower fees vs. DoorDash, but the exact delivery time; therefore, I ranked it marginally higher.

ENJOYABLE

An emotional vector that answers, "How easy was the end-to-end ordering and delivery experience?"

Assuming TastyDrone has a similar user experience to DoorDash and GrubHub, it all comes down to the actual enjoyment of the delivery.

GrubHub, DoorDash, Uber Eats, and every other company today deliver in the same way: a person drives up to your house, gets out of their car, puts a bag in front of your door, and drives off. TastyDrone is differentiated on this vector because they use drones instead of humans.

TastyDrone: 8

I ranked this vector for TastyDrone slightly higher because, in the early stages of growing the business, customers might find a drone delivering their food more enjoyable than a person dropping off a bag and driving away.

DoorDash and Grub Hub: 6

Enjoyment is relatively the same between DoorDash and GrubHub as a driver just dropped off the food in front of your door, and that's it.

CONNECTION

An emotional vector that answers, "How much of an emotional connection was created during the experience?"

Connection refers to the emotional attachment level of a person with a given brand. In the restaurant delivery space, there isn't much emotional connection. As such, I've scored all three relatively equally with low points.

TastyDrone: 3

I rate TastyDrone slightly higher since drones are the cornerstone of the experience. If another drone delivery company entered the space, we would not have any advantage against them in this regard.

DoorDash and GrubHub: 2

The relative emotional attachment someone has to DoorDash is almost the same as GrubHub because brands and experiences are relatively similar.

Next up, we'll have a look at indirect competitors and alternatives.

EXAMPLE #2: TASTYDRONE VS. INDIRECT COMPETITORS AND CURRENT ALTERNATIVES

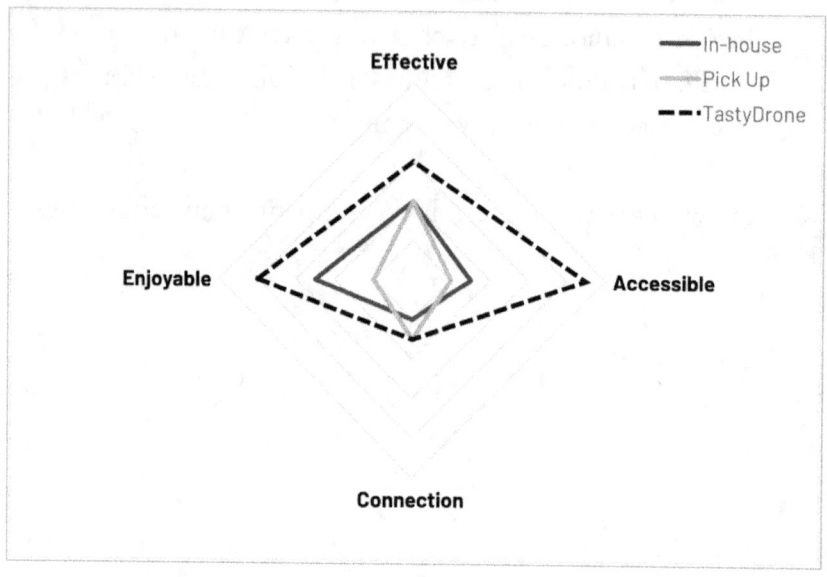

Above, TastyDrone is the same dashed black line as in the previous example. I swapped out DoorDash and GrubHub with in-house delivery drivers and the current alternative of driving to the restaurant to pick up your order. My scores for TastyDrone stay the same.

Here's the data:

Effective
TastyDrone: 6
In-house: 4
Pick Up: 4

Accessible

TastyDrone: 9
In-house: 3
Pick Up: 2

Enjoyable
TastyDrone: 8
In-house: 5
Pick Up: 2

Connection
TastyDrone: 3
In-house: 2
Pick Up: 3

I'll break down each of these scores again using the same framework I did last time.

EFFECTIVE

A logical vector that answers the question, "How correct was the order, and was it undamaged?"

TastyDrone can't do much about incorrect orders prepared at the restaurant. Still, they can try to ensure the drones themselves do not damage the food mid-flight.

TastyDrone: 6 Points
Almost every order arrives correctly and undamaged. But, TastyDrone could have an edge in not disturbing or damaging the order in transit. In contrast, cars and human drivers tend to have more turbulence than an even-keeled drone.

In-house and Pick Up: 4 Points

Because of DoorDash and GrubHub's quality assurance built into their platform to ensure orders are correct, I ranked them slightly higher than in-house delivery services. For the same reasons as in-house, opting to pick it up yourself will likely yield the same level of efficacy as in-house delivery drivers.

ACCESSIBLE

A logical vector that answers the question, "How fast did the order arrive, and how affordable was it?"

We know that accessibility is a linchpin vector, so we'll carefully consider this one when scoring indirect competitors and alternatives. In our last comparison, both DoorDash and GrubHub earned six points for accessibility as a reminder.

TastyDrone: 9

Again, due to the high speed and low cost of TastyDrone, I have rated TastyDrone higher than any direct and indirect competitors and current alternatives. I might rate this vector lower if another drone competitor entered the space with faster drones and lower fees.

In-house: 3

While in-house delivery fees are usually much lower than DoorDash or GrubHub, most restaurants have an app that speeds up ordering and delivery.

Pick Up: 2

Going to pick up the food yourself is the least convenient option, hence, I've given it the lowest accessibility score.

ENJOYABLE

An emotional vector that answers the question, "How easy was the end-to-end ordering and delivery experience?"

When comparing indirect competitors and current alternatives, the ease of ordering and the delivery experience takes on a slightly different flavor.

TastyDrone: 8
We're counting on the enjoyment factor of drone delivery and the same quick and easy ordering experience as DoorDash or GrubHub to keep the score high.

In-house: 5
Since most restaurants lack a food ordering app, I have rated in-house ordering slightly lower than TastyDrone and direct competitors but higher than pick up.

Pick Up: 2
Again, picking up the food yourself is the least convenient option.

CONNECTION

An emotional vector that answers the question, "How much of an emotional connection was created during the experience?"

When picking up your food yourself, restaurant customers get to interact with the restaurant staff and location more than they do would with DoorDash or GrubHub. Therefore there might be a greater chance for an emotional connection with a local restaurant.

TastyDrone: 3

The reason for this score is the same as last time; we haven't changed TastyDrone's overall score when comparing it to indirect competitors or current alternatives.

In-house: 2

Regular customers ordering from the same place repeatedly could have a slight emotional connection with their delivery driver, but that's it.

Pick Up: 3

When someone picks up food from a restaurant, they get to go into the location, say hi to the staff, and create more connection than a delivery drop-off.

BRINGING IT TOGETHER: STORYLINE COMPASS EVALUATION

Let's have one more look at the complete data table.

Effective
TastyDrone: 6
DoorDash: 5
GrubHub: 5
In-house: 4
Pick Up: 4

Accessible
TastyDrone: 9
DoorDash: 6
GrubHub: 7
In-house: 3
Pick Up: 2

Enjoyable
TastyDrone: 8
DoorDash: 6
GrubHub: 6
In-house: 5
Pick Up: 2

Connection
TastyDrone: 3
DoorDash: 2
GrubHub: 2
In-house: 2
Pick Up: 3

And the two compasses:

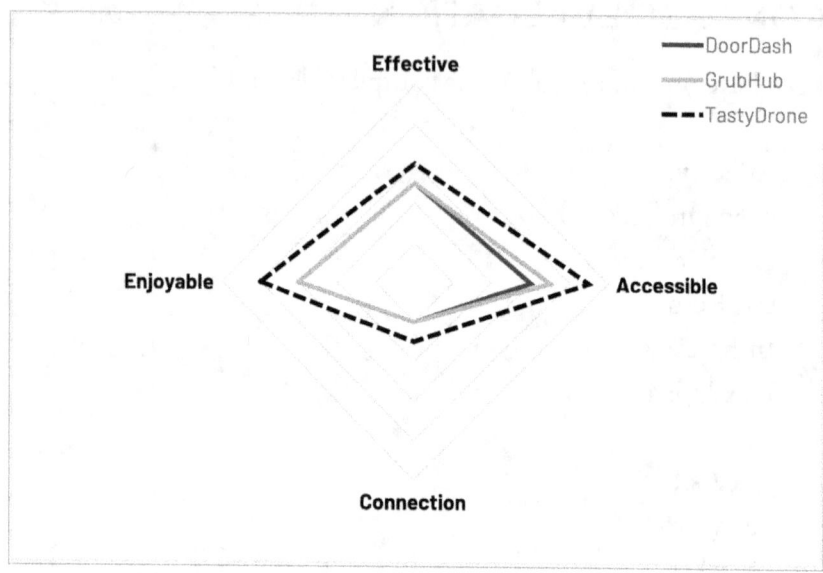

Direct Competitors

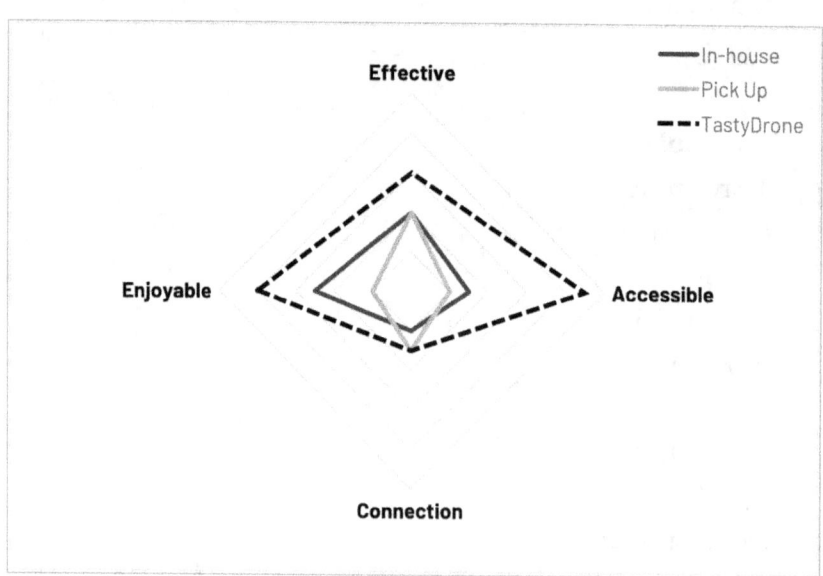

Indirect Competitors

In both cases above, we can see that TastyDrone has superior benefits across all four major vectors of the storyline compass.

Why the heck have we spent all this time doing so much subjective analysis? Read on!

CHAPTER 5
FOCUSING YOUR STARTUP'S STORY

COMPLETING the storyline compass exercise with direct competitors, indirect competitors, and current alternatives can provide startups with something they desperately need: *focus*.

A lack of focus is an immediate turn-off for investors. If you have any experience pitching to investors, you probably know that not seeming focused is a deal killer.

First, I'll show you an example of a pitch deck that isn't as focused as it could be. Then, I'll show you how the storyline compass can help focus that company and its efforts and how we can communicate that through the startup's pitch deck.

TASTYDRONE: AN EXAMPLE OF BEING SLIGHTLY UNFOCUSED

I've talked a lot about TastyDrone. This fictitious startup is off to a great start. They've progressed their software (the autonomous piloting element) and hardware (the proprietary drone docking stations). They've got some good early traction in the form of partner restaurants and pilot programs. They've even established solid strategic manufacturing partnerships to ramp up production when ready.

Up until now, the business's activities have been relatively focused. But, when pitching the story of TastyDrone to investors, it's all too easy to throw a bunch of unnecessary stuff in there that would de-rail that focus.

Let's assume the founders included the following content in their pitch. Each of these ideas on its own is a good idea. But, each is also a textbook pitch deck distraction that founders should carefully handle.

1. **Unfocused Expansion** - Launching in other cities before saturating or establishing great traction in the launch market of Austin, TX.
2. **Unfocused Payloads** - Expanding too early into the delivery of items other than restaurant delivery. Founders should save major vertical expansions for a few years down the road.
3. **Unfocused Marketing** - Focusing on mass consumer marketing too soon when direct-to-restaurant sales and experience should probably be the founder's priority.
4. **Unfocused Development** - Creating new features and functionality that don't directly contribute to nailing the fundamental differentiators of the startup (high-speed, low-cost take-out delivery), such as a communication platform for restaurant owners to re-market to their customers.
5. **Unfocused Revenue Streams** - Launching new revenue streams like a self-service advertising platform for local

restaurants might be a good idea in a few years. Still, it's unnecessary in the early stages of this startup.

Every idea above is relatively good, and the founders should consider each at some point in the company's growth. But, each of the above ideas also just happens to draw an investor's attention away from the core message and story.

How do we know what to include in our pitch deck and how to include it? The *linchpin vector* of our storyline compass helps with making these decisions.

USING THE LINCHPIN VECTOR TO SHARPEN FOCUS

Earlier, I mentioned the idea of a linchpin vector within the storyline compass. In this section, I'll define it, show you how to identify it, and demonstrate how to use it as a filter for your pitch.

As a reminder, the four major vectors in the storyline compass are effective, accessible, enjoyable, and emotional connection. Every possible benefit a company provides its customers can fall into one of these four vectors.

However, every company will have only one linchpin vector. The linchpin vector is the most important benefit category for that business to focus on. Knowing which of these vectors is the most important can become a handy filter for deciding what to do and what to talk about in your pitch deck.

Here are a few examples of linchpin vectors for startups:

Effective - It does a better job or gets better results:
Oura Ring (B2C) and The Trade Desk (B2B)

Accessible - It's easier, faster, or cheaper to get ahold of: Venmo (B2C) and SpaceX (B2B)

Enjoyable - It's prettier, more fun, or simpler to use: Uber (B2C) and Slack (B2B)

Connection - It provides more emotional value: Lulu's (B2C)

Business-to-Consumer Linchpin Vector Examples

Oura (ouraring.com) - The Oura ring is a wearable device that collects health data. It's similar to a Fitbit; only that it fits on your finger. In addition, the software offers helpful content to improve the wearer's overall health and life-style. Efficacy would be this company's linchpin vector. It does a better job of *collecting data on the wearer's health in a smaller package than a smartwatch.*

Venmo (venmo.com) - Venmo is a peer-to-peer payment provider that allows anyone to send money to anyone in a few taps. The main reason why people use the service is the near-instant transaction speed. It provides access to instant payments and nearly eliminates the need for cash or checks. As such, the linchpin vector for Venmo is *accessibility*. It's easier and faster to *send my friends money.*

Uber (uber.com) - Everyone knows Uber. While it may be cheaper to use Uber than a taxi and most definitely a car service, Uber isn't all about being the most affordable.

Uber's linchpin vector is *enjoyment*. They're about providing a more enjoyable *rider experience than traditional taxis.*

Lulu's (lulus.com) - Lulu's is a direct-to-consumer women's clothing brand. Like most fashion brands, Lulu's success depends on its emotional connection with potential buyers. Their linchpin vector is *emotional connection.* They win when they provide more emotional value to their customers through *the best clothing designs and branding for their audience.*

Business-to-Business Linchpin Vector Examples

The Trade Desk - (thetradedesk.com) The Trade Desk is a leading programmatic media buying and selling platform. For this category, keeping costs low while increasing the core performance metrics of online advertisers is everything. Here, the linchpin vector is *effectiveness.* They do a better job of getting better media results. Their entire value proposition revolves around buying and selling online advertising more efficiently and effectively.

SpaceX - (spacex.com) SpaceX is building a reusable launch platform to get more things into space faster at a lower cost. That places SpaceX's linchpin vector firmly in *accessibility.* They're making *space* easier, faster, and cheaper to access.

Slack - (slack.com) Slack provides a chat platform for

distributed and remote teams to collaborate more effec-tively. While their ultimate goal is to boost workplace productivity (something that the B2B buyers of Slack strongly emphasize), Slack is all about making communi-cation more enjoyable between teams. Slack's linchpin vector is *enjoyment*. Their platform is a much more enjoy-able *way to collaborate compared to email.*

N/A Emotional Connection - After thinking about this for a good while, I couldn't come up with any B2B companies that hung their entire reason-to-be on an emotional connection. Don't get me wrong, emotions play a big role in B2B decision-making. However, a lack of an example does mean that most B2B decisions would likely fall into one of the other vectors instead of being purely emotional. If you come up with any examples here, let me know, and I'll update this section and give you credit for the example.

LOGICAL VS. EMOTIONAL LINCHPIN VECTORS

It's important to note that out of the four different vectors, two are more logical, and two are more emotional. Effectiveness and accessibility can usually be measured quantitatively and don't require surveys to obtain KPIs that determine whether or not a business's solution is better or worse compared to competitors. On the other hand, enjoyment and emotional connection are more intangible. They require surveys or user interviews to deter-mine the extent of enjoyment or level of emotional connection created with customers.

Effectiveness and accessibility are 100% impacted by a company's product or service offering. Advertising will never make your solution more effective. To be more effective, you must improve your product. To be more accessible, you must make your product easier to access.

Enjoyability, however, is a hybrid between logical and emotional. But, what makes this an emotional vector is that enjoyment is intangible. You can only measure it by surveys, interviews, or user feedback.

The last one, emotional connection, literally has emotional in the title, but I shortened it to just "connection." If a customer chooses one brand over another simply because it's prettier or looks more like a brand that gets them, it's a purely emotional decision. Most companies that fall into this category are physical goods.

"Okay, Keane, so why is this important?"

By understanding the types of decision-making that contribute to a category's linchpin vector, businesses can further focus on activities that will most impact their customers' buying decisions.

If effectiveness is your startup's linchpin vector, this is a logical decision. Efforts that focus on influencing the emotional side of a customer's decision-making process won't go nearly as far as focusing on actions that improve how *effective* your startup's solution is.

Does that mean that branding and design don't matter? Nope. Branding is still a vital part of increasing credibility among your customers. But it does provide an additional layer of focus that can permeate your entire organization right down to your pitch deck.

Alternatively, if a company operates in a space governed by emotions, improving product effectiveness or accessibility (logical decisions) could be perceived as unfocused.

Does this mean focusing on product efficacy or accessibility doesn't matter? Again, nope. But, if a product is of too low quality, that will ultimately reflect poorly on the company, and long-term sales will suffer as word spreads in the form of negative reviews.

Should companies avoid spending money on advertising or sales? Obviously not! Driving awareness is fundamental to every business. But, understanding whether or not the decision-making process within a given category is logical or emotional can hone the relative weighting of efforts on a company's budget spreadsheet and in their pitch decks.

TARGET AUDIENCES AND LINCHPIN VECTORS

As mentioned previously, understanding the mindset of your target audience is essential to understanding how they make decisions.

Someone shopping for high-end yoga pants will have a completely different decision-making process than someone shopping for new enterprise resource planning (ERP) software for their company of thousands of global employees. The person shopping for premium yoga pants will care about quality, but their emotional connection with a brand will determine whether or not they buy from them. The person shopping for a new ERP tool will most likely care about accessibility-related benefits like low cost, speed of use, and the ability for employees to access it across multiple devices easily. However, the end-users of that ERP tool will most likely care about enjoyment. Therefore, for bifurcated audiences, there's a balancing act that startups need to play to meet the needs of end-users while communicating the right things to the buyers.

Furthermore, two target audiences within the same industry could have two different linchpin vectors. Let's look at the example of ride-share services again. Wealthier individuals might care more about the experience's enjoyment than how much it costs. As such, a luxury car service might not even look at low-cost ride-share services like Uber or Lyft as direct competitors. However, Uber does allow riders to select Uber Black, which provides premium and luxury vehicles. Therefore, a small part of Uber's offering does compete with luxury car services in that regard.

Is Uber unfocused by doing this? Not really. Uber launched this feature around 2014. Uber Black is the original Uber experience they launched in 2010. They started calling it Uber Black when they launched UberX, the more "everyday" rideshare service we're all used to nowadays.

But what if a luxury car service startup is in its first year of operation and wants to launch a low-cost offering? Is that unfocused? Most likely, yes. Companies in their early stages of growth should still focus on nailing their core offering within their launch target's linchpin vector. Only after several years of consistent market share growth in their launch market should they consider expanding to another target market.

REMINDER: DOWNLOAD THE FREE COMPANION KIT!

If you haven't already, you'd want to download the supplementary documents that expand on the concepts in this book.

Visit This Link To Download:
https://stry.pro/hgkit

Included in the kit:
Before-after pitch decks
One-page cheat sheets
Printable worksheets
Resources and links

CHAPTER 6
REFOCUSING YOUR DECK

Now that you've learned how the storyline compass can focus your startup's efforts, I'll go over how to use the compass to shape your entire pitch deck's story. In general, each of the four different vectors of the storyline compass requires certain elements to be present or omitted when creating your pitch.

Here's a rough overview of how each vector should come to life in a pitch:

More Effective

- Show tangible, measured proof of greater efficacy
- Show your efficacy data vs. the competition

More Accessible

- Establish inaccessibility of competition

- Show proof you're more accessible vs. the competition

More Enjoyable

- Prove that enjoyability is the linchpin for winning
- Establish the level of enjoyment for the competition
- Show tangible proof that you are more enjoyable

More Connection

- Prove that emotional connection is the linchpin for winning
- Establish the level of an emotional connection vs. the competition
- Show evidence that you can/are establishing a greater connection

As mentioned, a company's storyline compass and linchpin vectors will change based on its business model. B2C and D2C startups will need to focus more on accessibility, enjoyment, and emotional connection, while B2B startups will need to focus much more on effectiveness, accessibility, and enjoyment. Use the below list as a general guide to determining your startup's potential linchpin vectors.

- **More Effective:** B2C and B2B Tech
- **More Accessible:** B2C Marketplaces and B2B Marketplaces
- **More Enjoyable:** B2C Tech, D2C Products, B2B Tech
- **More Connection:** D2C Products

Notice how most business models deprioritize achieving more emotional connection. It doesn't make sense for every business. If you're a B2B SaaS startup launching with the idea that branding alone will allow you to become a successful contender in the space, you're probably wrong.

The only business model that aims to forge a more emotional connection is with consumer brands. Most of these buying decisions are quick and frequent. Consumer branding is about creating an emotional connection, which is why the multi-billion-dollar advertising industry exists. For most products and brands to stand out to a consumer, the consumer must first experience an emotional connection. For every other business model type, creating a business that focuses on creating an emotional connection isn't as important as efficacy, accessibility, or enjoyment.

Remember that the scores in this book are subjective, and there will be exceptions. Regardless, the above table can be a fantastic guide if you're building a business that fits into one of these categories.

DRILLING INTO PITCH DECK SPECIFICS

Now it's time to get into the nitty-gritty. This section will dive into our recommended framework for early-stage pitch decks, and will also pinpoint precisely what you need to change or modify in your pitch deck to align with the storyline compass for your startup.

At STORY, we look at most pitch decks as having three major sections: the upfront, the current state, and the future state. We use a 15-slide framework and adjust this based on the type of business and its current maturity state.

We can break those 15 slides into 42 story elements that most pitch decks need to include. Two-thirds of those story elements (66%) are affected by a business's storyline compass and linchpin vector.

Here are the elements affected by the storyline compass, noted with a ✓ mark.

UPFRONT - Deck Intro Slides

TITLE: Startup Name ✓, Hook ✓, Benefit Statement ✓, Social Proof ✓

TREND: Your Category, Category Market Sizes, Category Market Growth, Geographic Focus, Category Trends/Drivers ✓

PROBLEM: Your Target Customer, Their Problems ✓, Data About Those Problems

SOLUTION: Your Benefits ✓, Your Features ✓

CURRENT STATE - Middle Meat of the Deck

TRACTION: Founding Date, Quantitative Achievements ✓, Qualitative Achievements ✓

MODEL: Primary Revenue Stream ✓, Primary Stream Economics ✓, Additional Streams ✓

HOW IT WORKS: Primary Product/Service ✓,

Primary Features ✓, Additional Products/Services and their Features ✓

ADVANTAGE: Your Direct Competition ✓, Your Indirect Competition ✓, How You're Better ✓

FUTURE STATE - What's Next / Outro slides

GO-TO-MARKET: Y1 Goal/KPI/Growth Tactics ✓, Y2 Goal/KPI/Growth Tactics ✓, Y3 Goal/KPI/Growth Tactics ✓

OPPORTUNITY: Target Annual Opportunity, Expansion Opportunities

VISION / ROADMAP: The Big Vision ✓, When You'll Achieve It, Timeline of Future Evolution ✓

TEAM / ADVISORS: Team ✓, Advisors ✓

FINANCIALS: 3-5 Year P&L Statement

USE OF FUNDS: How Much You're Raising, How You'll Spend It ✓, Over How Long, What Will It Help Achieve ✓

WHY NOW: Why Is Now The Best Time ✓, What 3 Things The Investor Should Remember ✓

To show you how this comes to life, I'll use TastyDrone once again.

STRENGTHENING YOUR PITCH: TASTYDRONE EXAMPLE

As a brief reminder, here are the storyline compasses we put together for TastyDrone.

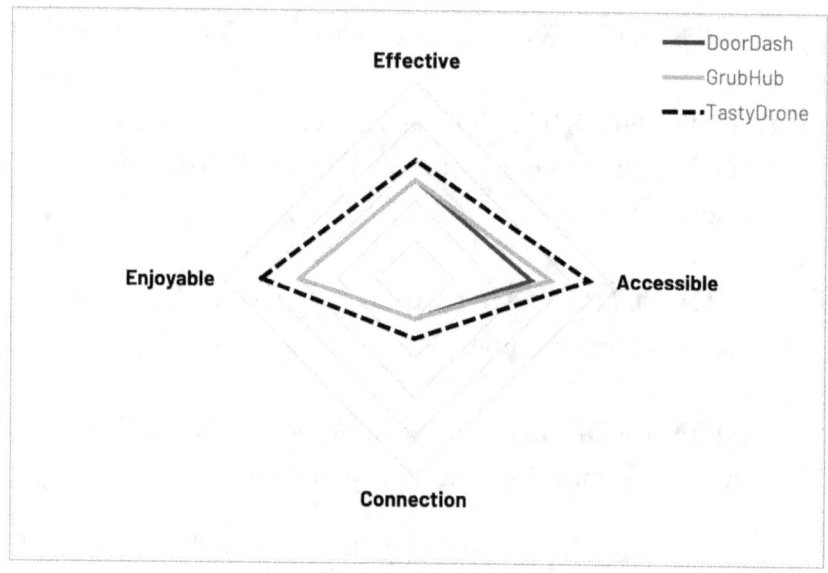

Direct Competitors

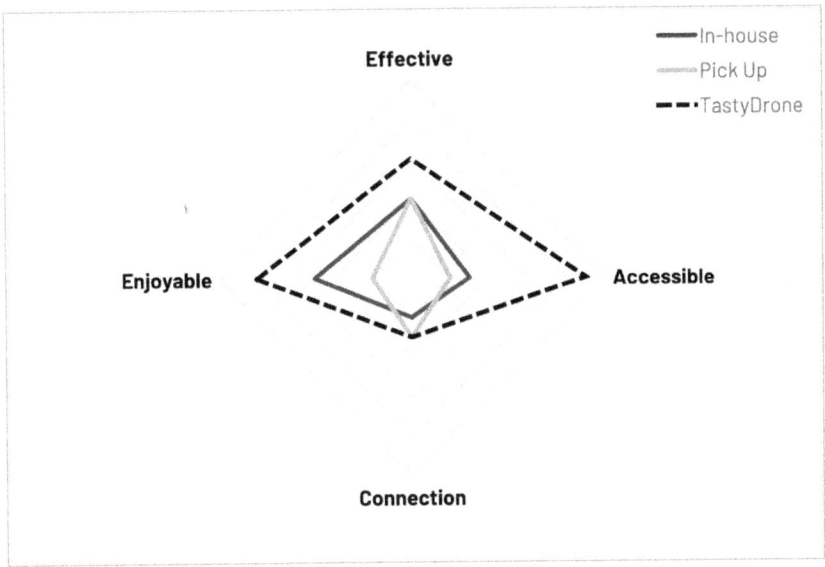

Indirect Competitors

The linchpin vector we decided on for TastyDrone was accessibility, specifically *faster delivery speeds, and lower delivery fees.*

Now we'll review every element impacted by the storyline compass and ensure that we align our messaging for each aligns with the linchpin vector of our compass.

Reminder: TastyDrone is a fake company. The data I'm using for this example is also fictitious.

TITLE SLIDE

The title slide is the very first slide of your deck. It acts like a billboard for your company and has one purpose: to get investors to keep reading. Founders can achieve this effect by nailing a combination of elements. Now, let's go over each.

Startup Name ✓[1]

You may not have guessed that this book would have a tiny section about how to name your startup, but it is vital that were communicating the right things starting with the name of the startup itself.

Compass Implications: We should emphasize speed and convenience. Since we achieve that with drones, we should consider including that in the name. Lastly, we could talk about low cost, but usually, brands with something about low cost seem cheap (e.g., Costco, Dollar Store, etc.), and we want to avoid that.

Bad Example: "*Yummeal*" This name doesn't mention speed or convenience and instead leans into enjoyability. Also, it doesn't mention drones!

Good Example: "*TastyDrone*" The word "tasty" is in there but implies food with the bonus of deliciousness, while "drone" is very straightforward in that it means we use drones.

Hook ✓

The hook is what we call the investor tagline. It's a short statement that hints at what the startup does in a few words. Its job is to make investors want to keep reading. Usually, it goes right below your logo on the title slide.

Compass Implications: Since this is all about effectiveness (get here fast) and accessibility (make it cheap), we'll lean into those. But we also know that enjoyment is a factor (easy ordering, has the restaurants I want, etc.), so we might consider peppering that in.

Bad Examples: *"Local delivery by drone."* This hook focuses on localness, but speed and cost are the most important.

"Fly the delicious skies." This hook focuses on deliciousness, but speed and lower cost are the most important.

Good Examples: *"TastyDrone it for less."* This hook loosely works but still leaves the reader guessing too much about what we do.

"Eat on the fly for less." This hook emphasizes speed and lower cost, and we get the double meaning of "on the fly."

Benefit Statement ✓

A benefit statement is a short, seven- to ten-word sentence below the hook on your title slide. It describes what the business does more directly to eliminate any questions the hook may raise. We'll use this benefit statement at the top of our solution slide in the first part of a pitch deck and again on our last slide.

Compass Implications: Our benefit statement needs to speak to speed and affordability.

Bad Examples: *"Delighting restaurant delivery customers with a breakthrough drone delivery platform."* A benefit statement like this focuses on delight, emphasizing enjoyability, which isn't a priority.

"Making restaurant delivery amazing with a scalable drone platform." This statement focuses on making restaurant delivery "amazing," which is subjective and emotional. However, our linchpin vector is steering us toward the more logical vector of accessibility: high speed and low cost, and this benefit statement speaks to neither.

Good Examples: *"Making restaurant delivery faster and more affordable with a scalable drone platform."* This one is bang on about speed and cost, and it implies who are target audience is and what our technology is. We've got a ton of focused information using just 85 characters.

"Fast, affordable delivery with a proprietary drone platform." This statement is a remixed version of the first one, broadening the scope of what the business is trying to do. It does this by omitting the word "restaurant" or "meal" from this and instead says "delivery." It also leaves room for us to speak to vertical expansion beyond food.

Social Proof ✓

When creating title slides for companies with more traction, we try including social proof on the first slide. One way to do this is by including award, press, or investor logos. If the business has them, we could also include a customer testimonial.

Compass Implications: Our linchpin vector is accessibility (high-speed, low-cost), so we need to show a quote that reinforces this.

Bad Example: "*I love TastyDrone! Seeing that little guy land with my tacos is so cute!*" This customer quote focuses on emotional delight, which goes against our linchpin vector.

Good Example: "*TastyDrone is affordable and gets there fast. It's perfect for our growing restaurant.*" This ideal testimonial is from a restaurant participating in our fictitious beta program. It reinforces how restaurants benefit from our solution.

Bringing It Together: Title Slide

Company
TastyDrone

Hook
Eat on the fly for less.

Benefit Statement
Fast, affordable delivery with a proprietary drone platform.

Social Proof
"*TastyDrone is affordable and gets there fast. It's perfect for our growing restaurant.*" —TastyDrone Beta Customer

**TastyDrone gets food delivery profitable
with a scalable, AI-drone delivery network.**

As featured by:

Forbes   BUSINESS INSIDER   **Inc.**

Investor Pitch Deck – Q2 2021

This is an example pitch deck for a fake company prepared for the **Startup Power Pitch Online Course** by STORYPitchDecks.com

Original Title Slide

Updated Title Slide

---

1. The checkmark signifies that this part of your pitch deck is impacted by the storyline compass.

TREND SLIDE

We usually recommend starting pitch decks out with a trend slide. A trend slide early on orients investors to the industry you'll be discussing and informs them of the primary market trend you're watching. It shows that you've done your homework and you're thinking about the bigger picture.

None of the below elements impact your storyline compass. Instead, they should inform it:

- **Your Category** - The industry or sector your startup operates in
- **Geographic Focus** - The region your startup operates in
- **Category Market Sizes** - The current total market size in volume or revenue of your category
- **Category Market Growth** - The growth rate of your industry expressed in compound annual growth rate and typically abbreviated as CAGR

Category Trends/Drivers ✓

The only element that your storyline compass affects on the trend slide is the category or industry trend that is relevant to your startup and the macroeconomic forces that underpin those trends.

Compass Implications: Trends should align and shed light on the linchpin vectors for the category. In this example, our linchpin vector of accessibility means we must emphasize high delivery speeds and low delivery costs for end users.

Bad Example: "91% of delivery app users also use ride-share apps like Uber." Here, we're way off-topic. Bringing up this point on the first slide is irrelevant because we have no reason to. Bringing it up on a later slide is also irrelevant. We shouldn't include this point in our deck as it doesn't inform any of our critical decisions as a company.

Good Example: "87% of all restaurants use a restaurant delivery app because it's what 95% of what customers want" This data demonstrates the need for the category is still strong. It's a good setup point, but it might not be strong enough alone.

"80% of delivery app downloads are from younger suburbanites with two-thirds of 18-29-year-olds having used one in the last 90 days" When combined with the above data point, we get a complete picture of what's going on in this category. We also get the added benefit of bringing up both the restaurants and the customers, our two end-users.

Bringing It Together: Trend Slide

Your Category
Online Restaurant Delivery Services

Geographic Focus
United States

Market Sizes

The US Online Food Delivery market is worth $22.4 billion in 2023

Market Growth

Revenue is expected to show an annual growth rate (CAGR 2023-2029) of 11%, resulting in a projected market volume of $320B by 2029

Category Trends Or Drivers

• 87% of all restaurants use a restaurant delivery app because it's what 95% of what customers want.
• 80% of delivery app downloads are from younger suburbanites with two-thirds of 18-29-year-olds having used one in the last 90 days.

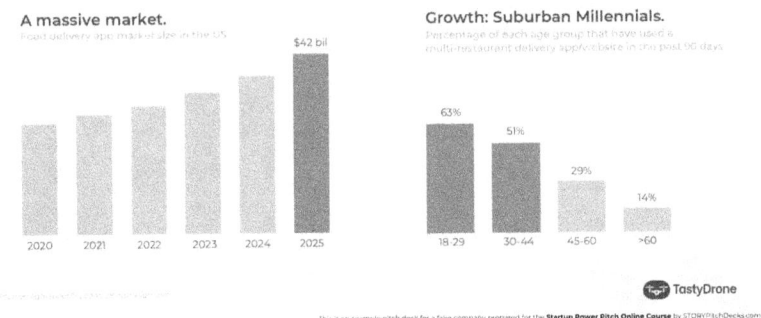

Original Trend Slide

Updated Trend Slide

PROBLEM SLIDE

I'm a firm believer in using just a single problem slide. In less than 5% of pitch decks, founders might need to include a second problem slide. We only do this when a complex category requires more investor education. Biotech is a good example of an exception. However, most startups should aim for just one clear, uncluttered problem slide.

The below content is not affected by your storyline compass. Instead, it should inform it:

- **Your Target Customer** - Who you sell your solution to and who ultimately uses it

Their Problems ✓

The problem statements you choose to include in your pitch deck are super important. They should be short and limited to no more than three. Occasionally, we'll include data on the problem slide, but we've seen great success in limiting the content to just the problem statements.

Compass Implications: The problem slide is where aligning your story to the linchpin vector of your storyline compass counts most. The problems we discuss for our end-users must align with low-cost and high-speed delivery. All we need to do is invert those two benefits, and we'll get our problems: high cost and the inversion of high-speed delivery is slow delivery.

Bad Example: "*Customers complain about incorrect orders*" While this problem may be accurate, it doesn't align with speed or cost.

Good Example: "*The average meal delivery app charges 50% in fees per order and takes over 60 minutes to arrive.*" Here, we're right on the money about speed and cost (pun intended).

"*99% of delivery app users want lower fees, and 75% complain about slow delivery times.*" This data is somewhat custom, and the founders would likely need to run a short survey to get it, but it would be instrumental in shedding additional light on the problem.

Bringing It Together: Problem Slide

Target Customer
Suburban millennial customers and small restaurants

Their Problems
• Price-gouging, high fees
• Takes too long to arrive
• Yet, everyone still uses them!

Data About Those Problems
• 99% of restaurants and customers want lower delivery fees while 75% complain about slow delivery
• The average delivery markup fee is 50% with the average delivery time at one hour

Original Problem Slide

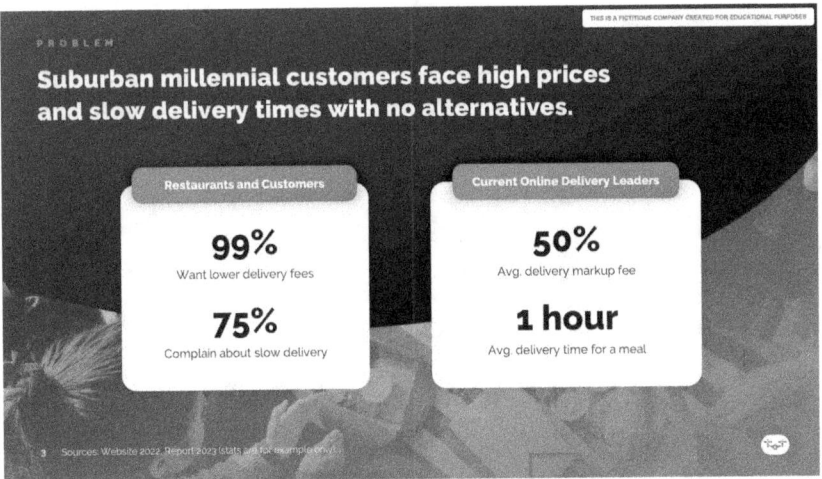

Updated Problem Slide

SOLUTION SLIDE

The solution slide always follows the problem slide. One of the main things the solution slide must do is directly address each of the problems laid out on our problem slide. The good news is we already know our benefits, low cost, and high speed, and we engineered the problem slide to discuss both.

Your Benefits ✓

The benefit statement prepared for our title slide is overarching, but the solution slide requires founders to go deeper. We don't recommend more than three benefit statements on this solution slide. Founders should also pair each benefit with a feature. Writing these statements is straightforward, as we've already worked out our storyline compass and linchpin vectors. Consequently, we are already crystal clear on what these benefits are.

Compass Implications: We must address slow speeds and high costs as laid out on the previous problem slide. We will handle speed first, followed by fees. It will always be in the same order throughout the deck.

Bad Example: "We deliver food and smiles with drones." Beyond being super cringe, the word "smiles" speaks to enjoyment and emotional connection, which doesn't address the problem laid out.

Good Example: "*We are twice as fast (30 min vs. 60) at half the cost (25% fees vs. 50%)*" These points speak directly to speed and cost. If we can include comparison stats or data on the solution, that is usually preferred.

Your Features ✓

A business's features are the mechanisms that create value and benefit the end user. We'll limit this to three main features for our solution slide and ensure we pair each with a benefit.

Compass Implications: Whatever features we discuss, we must align these with faster delivery and lower fees. These features are the engine that makes TastyDrone's benefits possible.

Bad Example: "*Cutting edge drone technology.*" Cool, but this doesn't explain how TastyDrone achieves cheaper and faster delivery.

Good Examples: "*We use scalable and patented docking stations in combination with off-the-shelf long-range drones and our proprietary AI piloting software.*" We usually list no more than three features for simplicity and clarity. We also check that each feature statement has roughly the same number of characters. This copy standardization ensures that the slide looks aesthetically pleasing once designed.

Bringing It Together: Solution Slide

Company
TastyDrone

Hook
Eat on the fly for less.

Benefit Statement
Fast, affordable delivery with a proprietary drone platform.

Benefits
- Half the cost, 25% fees vs. 50%
- Twice as fast, 30 min vs. 60 min

Features
- Scalable, patented docking stations
- Off-the-shelf long-range drones
- Proprietary AI piloting software

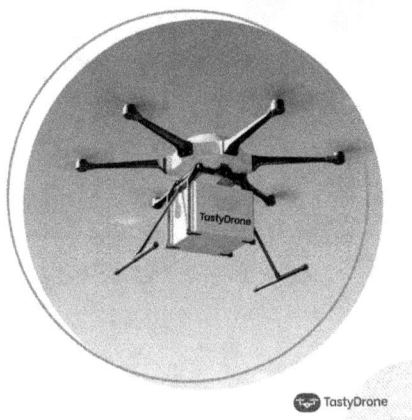

SOLUTION

TastyDrone gets food delivery profitable with a scalable, AI-drone delivery network.
● ● ●

PROFITABLE MODEL
Removes manual labor from delivery

SCALABLE NETWORK
Proprietary AI hardware and software

TastyDrone

Updated Problem Slide

Updated Solution Slide

WRAPPING UP THE UPFRONT

Awesome! So far, we've got the content for our title, trend, problem, and solution slides. All of these have been written and optimized to our storyline compass. Now it's time to move on to the middle meat of the deck, where we can dive into more detail about the business.

TRACTION SLIDE

The traction slide is where to highlight your achievements. Only the most important milestones you've met should be on this slide. It's always best if founders can tell this story objectively using data.

Quantitative Achievements ✓

While we wouldn't write "quantitative achievements" on a slide, this element's content is numerical.

Compass Implications: There may be metrics beyond the linchpin vectors that require discussion. Ideally, the metrics we include should speak to lower costs and improved speed of delivery. Founders should always build data collection and testing into their early-stage pilots and tests, even if they haven't officially launched the business.

Bad Example: "*One hour, long-range battery life.*" We wouldn't be aligned with our high-speed and low-cost linchpin vectors if we included a stat on battery life. If we want to talk about battery life, we must keep it in the context of delivery speed.

Good Examples: "*$10 average revenue per delivery and $7 average profit per delivery*" It's best to demonstrate this with a chart showing revenue and operating margins since launch. We could even forecast this out a few years to show margins increasing as we add more docking stations and drones.

"Our average delivery time is 15 minutes, 50% faster than DoorDash." Pilot or test programs will be essential to prove that our technology can first go to a location, retrieve its payload, deliver it, and return to a base station for charging, and second do all that autonomously, quickly, and without accidents.

"10 Pilot Restaurant Locations" This stat does a few things. First, it says that the company has tested its technology in the real world. Second, it provides a sense of where the business is regarding development. Ten locations aren't much, but it's a great place to start.

Qualitative Achievements ✓

Again, I wouldn't write this on a slide, but this element focuses on communicating the accomplishments we can't translate into data points.

Compass Implications: Keeping our linchpin vector in mind, we should align these just like we did with the quantitative achievements; to high speed and low cost.

Bad Example: *"Our drones are produced by the leading drone manufacturer in China!"* A statement like this is probably important to bring up at some point, but it's less critical given our linchpin vector is about accessibility for the end customer. As long as the drones work and are reasonably economical, it doesn't matter who made them.

Good Examples: *"We've got an initial signed LOI from Starbucks!"* Obtaining an LOI from a big company like Starbucks is huge and should be called out on the company's traction slide in big, bold text.

"Hardware and software patents filed." Showing off what you've done to protect your hard work legally is always a good thing, regardless of your linchpin vector.

Bringing It Together: Traction Slide

Quantitative Achievements
- Founded Q1 2020
- Raised $500k Pre-Seed, Q1'22
- 2 Austin, TX Pilots Conducted, Q3'22
- 4 Prototype Drones In Operation
- 100 Deliveries Made In Pilot Test

Qualitative Achievements
- Founding Team Established
- Manufacturing Partner Contracted
- Patents Filed for Software/Hardware
- Initial LOI signed from Starbucks

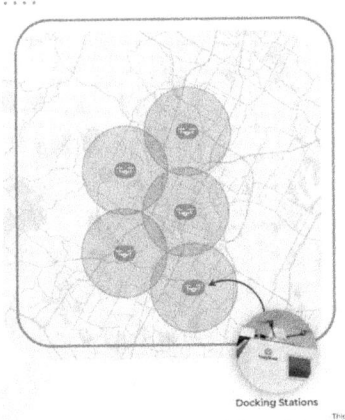

TRACTION

In Q4, TastyDrone delivered 2,412 meals with an average delivery time of 12 minutes.

Austin, TX Pilot
— Q4 2020
— 15 mile radius
— 50x drones
— 5x docking stations
— 25 restaurants

Results
2,412 meals delivered
12 min avg delivery time
98% delivery success

Docking Stations

TastyDrone

This is an example pitch deck for a fake company prepared for the **Startup Power Pitch Online Course** by STORYPitchDecks.com

Original Traction Slide

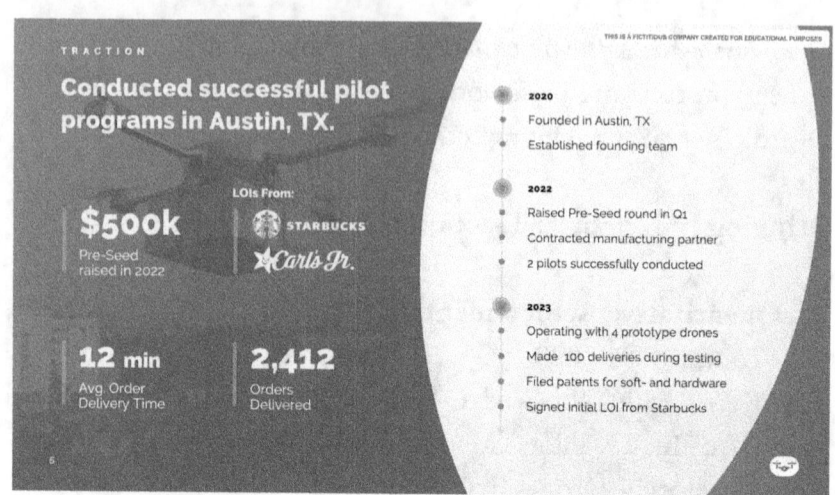

Updated Traction Slide

MODEL SLIDE

The model slide outlines how a startup makes money. We usually put this right after the traction slide or directly following a few product slides. At a high level, this slide should have your products and how you've priced them. If you'd like to take it a step further, you can show operating margins or a chart explaining how your model scales in revenue over time.

Primary Revenue Stream ✓

For pre-revenue companies, having a simple business model with the bulk of your cash flow originating from a single source is imperative. If you are the founder of a pre-revenue company and are considering more than two revenue streams, I recommend trimming them back and focusing on the one that will drive most of your revenue in the short term.

Compass Implications: TastyDrone earns revenue when people order takeout delivery. Here is where the rubber meets the road for our linchpin vector of low cost. Low cost here doesn't just mean it costs less for the consumer and the restaurant; it also means low cost for TastyDrone because drones are more affordable than humans.

Bad Example: "We plan to launch restaurant delivery at the same time we launch local small parcel delivery." Bad idea. This approach is a classic case of an early-stage company trying to do too much at once. It also doesn't address our high-speed, low-cost restaurant delivery linchpin vectors.

Good Examples: "*We charge a flat $5 fee per drone to customers and restaurants for a total of $10 in revenue per delivery. One drone can carry roughly one meal.*" This point shows how much the end users will pay to use the service and our revenue per delivery. We can also visualize that larger orders require more drones to deliver them, so even though we use a flat model, it still scales alongside order volume.

"*As we add more drones and docking stations to our network, TastyDrone's delivery speed increases and our cost per delivery decreases.*" This content is the icing on the linchpin vector cake. It shows how speed and cost are tied together and achieve network effects as we grow.

Additional Streams ✓

Additional revenue streams increase a company's income but are not necessarily the primary revenue drivers. Though founders should note that this is more appropriate for Series-A and above companies. Earlier-stage companies should focus on fewer revenue streams.

Compass Implications: Here is where we'd talk about other ways to earn revenue. In the future, we may consider other options, such as small parcel last-mile delivery, but we'll save that for the roadmap, opportunity, or vision slides.

Bad Example: "*We're also working on an advertising platform where local businesses can attach a banner to each drone.*" We must stay focused, and discussing resource spending on something we shouldn't be thinking about now isn't focused.

Good Example: "*Customers can turbocharge their order and expedite delivery for an additional $5 fee.*" This revenue stream still falls very close to the primary revenue stream of takeout delivery. It's more of an upsell, but it works because it shows that we can make our fast service *even faster* for a fee.

Bringing It Together: Model Slide

Primary Revenue Stream
• Flat $5 fee/drone for customers and restaurants ($10.00 total/drone)
• One drone = One meal

Additional Revenue Streams
• $5 TurboCharge fee to expedite delivery

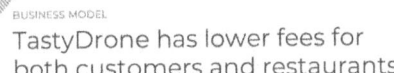

BUSINESS MODEL

TastyDrone has lower fees for both customers and restaurants.

Bigger orders = more drones:
Order via the app
$5 customer fee / order
$5 restaurant fee / order
$25 order minimum

Drones service a 6 mi radius:
$900 per drone
$5,000 per docking station
10x drones per station
2 sq mi overlap

 TastyDrone

This is an example pitch deck for a fake company prepared for the **Startup Power Pitch Online Course** by STORYPitchDecks.com

Original Model Slide

Updated Model Slide

HOW IT WORKS SLIDE

The "How it works" section explains in a little bit more detail how your products or services work. Usually, this section is anywhere between one and three slides maximum.

Primary Product/Service And Features ✓ - Whatever product or service we listed as the primary revenue driver on the model slide is what we should talk about here. For TastyDrone, this means explaining the end-to-end drone delivery process in more detail.

Compass Implications: The previous slide focused on the economics of our business. Conversely, these slides cover the operational side. How it works slides (also referred to as product slides), focus on how the company fulfills its promise of high-speed, low-cost delivery. These slides are also where founders should solve any questions about model scalability. Scalability has nothing to do with a linchpin vector or our storyline compass, but it's something that most investors want to see.

Bad Example: *"Seeing a drone deliver your food is the most fun experience possible! Each delivery has four major steps, and here's how we ensure each step is as enjoyable as possible."* Fun and enjoyment aren't linchpin vectors.

Good Example: *"Our proprietary docking stations scale quickly across geographic areas, and our AI piloting software calculates the fastest routes."* This sentence speaks to delivery speed and scale. It also manages to sneak in points about proprietary hardware and software, which makes TastyDrone faster and more affordable than competitors. Here, it might also be best to show some process graphics. This slide can also address how each element keeps TastyDrone's delivery costs as low as possible.

Additional Products/Services And Their Features ✓

Again, for early-stage companies, there shouldn't be many other products or services. But, TastyDrone could take another slide or two to represent how their primary offering works visually.

Compass Implications: For TastyDrone, the three main elements of their product are:

1. Proprietary docking stations
2. Off-the-shelf long-range drones
3. AI drone piloting software

When we talk about each of the above, each should always emphasize speed and cost for both our customers and TastyDrone. Writing these slides will be a delicate balance because adding too much information to the slide will dilute its potency.

Bad Example: *"Our AI piloting algorithm is so sophisticated. Here are three more slides that explain it in great detail!"* This mistake is one we see with technical founders. They love to talk about their product, how cool it is, and how they solved complex problems along the way. Put these in an appendix or remove them from the deck and only elaborate if asked.

Good Examples: _"Our proprietary docking stations double each drone's range, our city-wide networks cut time-to-delivery speeds in half, and a single technician can oversee hundreds of drones in an area."_ These three bullets add some additional color about how our product works, but notice how each point emphasizes speed and cost for everyone. The last point discusses how the whole thing is mostly hands-off and requires minimal maintenance.

Bringing It Together: How It Works Slide

Primary Product
Our proprietary docking stations scale quickly across areas, and our AI piloting software ensures the fastest routes.

The Process
1. Customer Orders via App
2. Restaurant Prepares Order
3. Drones Dispatched and Loaded
4. Drones Deliver Then Recharge

Key Features
• Proprietary docking stations double each drone's range.
• City-wide networks cut time-to-delivery speeds in half.
• One technician can oversee hundreds of drones in an area.

Our proprietary docking stations and and AI piloting program are patented.

Docking stations
Built with tech partner in China
Each charges and docks 10 drones

Hands-off AI
Coded and tested over 2 years
Can pilot 10,000+ drones at once

 TastyDrone

This is an example pitch deck for a fake company prepared for the **Startup Power Pitch Online Course** by STORYPitchDecks.com

Original How It Works Slide

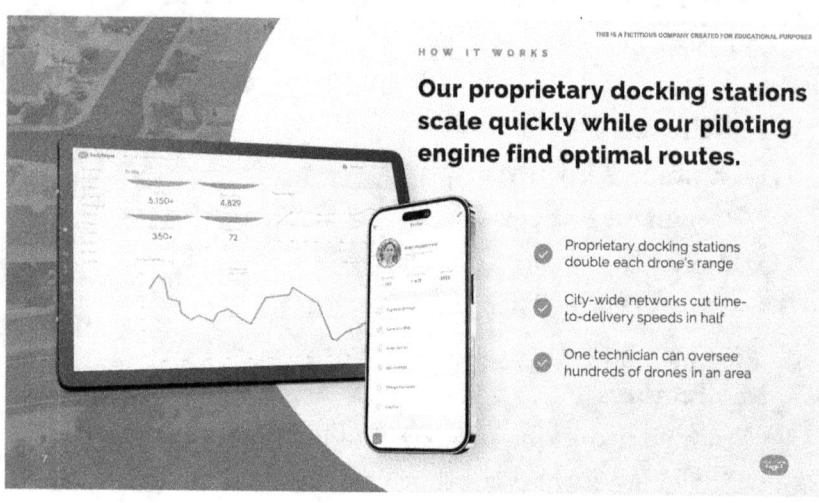

Updated How It Works Slide #1

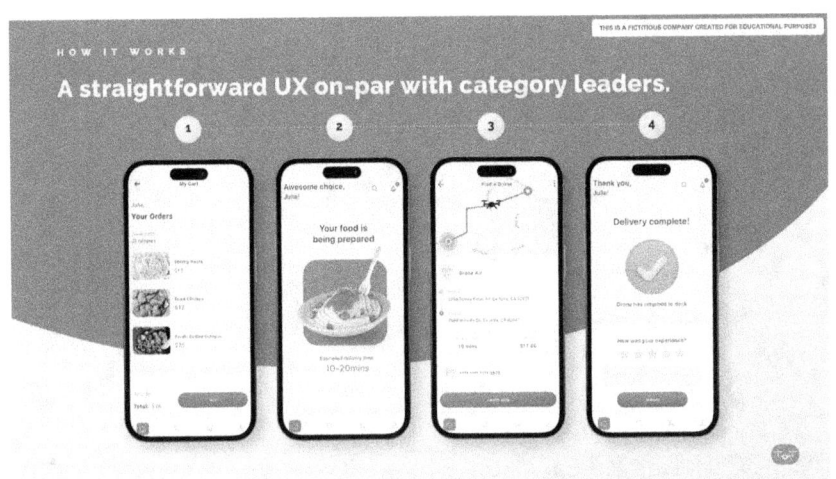

Updated How It Works Slide #2

ADVANTAGE SLIDE

The advantage slide is where we talk about the competition. We also call it the landscape slide. Its main purpose is to showcase the company's relative positioning and advantage versus direct and indirect competitors. Typically, we use a four-box, feature-function matrix, or other visual on this slide.

Your Direct Competition ✓

Direct competitors fight for the same dollar your business does. Usually, their solution is similar or somewhat similar to yours.

Compass Implications: Direct competitors also typically compete on the same linchpin vectors as your business. In this case, it's high-speed (even if they aren't as fast as TastyDrone) and low cost (even if they may cost more than TastyDrone).

Bad Example: "*Our direct competitors include meal-in-a-box services like Hello Fresh.*" When a person is hungry and orders from DoorDash, that's the dollar TastyDrone is competing for. TastyDrone isn't competing for the dollars a person may spend going to the grocery store.

Good Example: "*Our direct competitors include DoorDash, GrubHub, Uber Eats, and DroneX.*" We'd show some sort of visual with this statement explaining how each competitor has positioned itself across a few different variables. DroneX is a brand I made up, but here is where TastyDrone should mention other early-stage drone delivery startups if they exist.

Your Indirect Competition ✓

Earlier in the book, I discussed the concept of indirect competition. To reiterate, indirect competitors may compete for the same dollar your business does, but their solution significantly differs from yours.

Compass Implications: Indirect competitors fight for the same dollar as you, but they might have a different target or linchpin vector that's more important for their business.

Bad Example: "*Our indirect competition includes frozen meals at the grocery store.*" DoorDash doesn't look at frozen microwavable meals as competition, nor should TastyDrone.

Good Example: "*We look at traditional in-house delivery drivers as indirect competition, but we plan on rolling out a service where restaurants can pay for a dedicated docking station and drones.*" Restaurants with delivery drivers on staff are expensive, but they're probably not as expensive as having a drone army to handle rush hour. In the future, these restaurants could become TastyDrone customers.

How You're Better ✓

How your company is better than your competition are your key differentiators. If you omit them, investors will ask about them, so include them as bullet points on this slide.

Compass Implications: Obviously, this is all about our linchpin vector. Each differentiator should speak to higher speeds and lower costs. Bonus points if they include protected intellectual property or operational scalability.

Bad Example: "Our app experience is far superior to DoorDash or Uber Eats." While I find it hard to believe that a small development team could create a better UX than billion-dollar global technology companies, it is irrelevant because a better app experience (enjoyment) is not a linchpin vector.

Good Examples: "TastyDrone's platform achieves 50% faster delivery times, 50% lower customer fees, and 80% cheaper operating costs, with patent-pending in-house IP." These points speak to high speed, low cost, more scalability, and intellectual property protection. It's a quadruple-slam-dunk.

Bringing It Together: Advantage Slide

Direct Competition
DoorDash, GrubHub, Uber Eats, DroneX

Indirect Competition
Traditional in-house delivery drivers on staff at restaurants

Key Differentiators
• 50% faster delivery times
• 50% lower customer fees
• 80% cheaper operating costs
• Patent-pending in-house IP

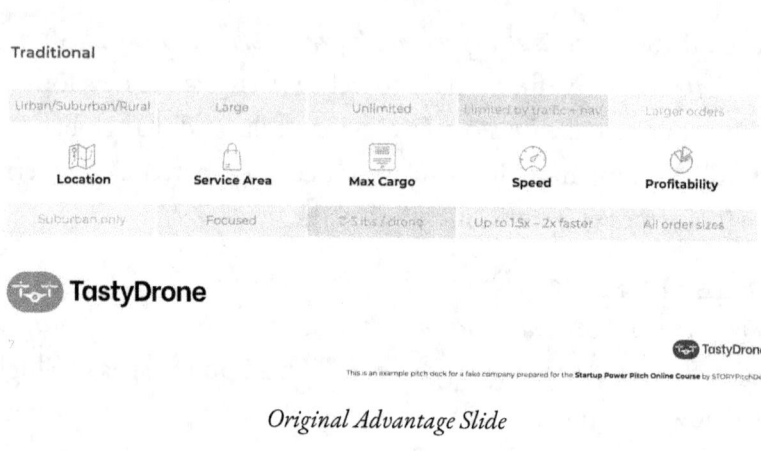

Original Advantage Slide

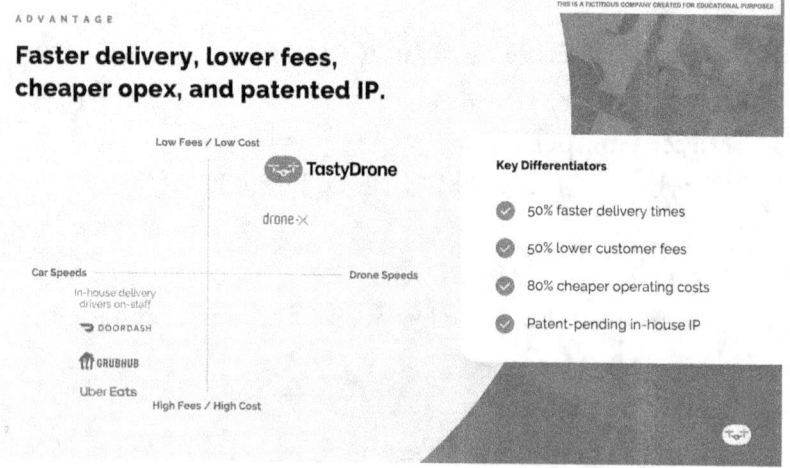

Updated Advantage Slide

WRAPPING UP CURRENT STATE

Sweet! We now have content for our traction, business model, how it works, and competitive advantage slides. Let's move on to the last section of our pitch deck, which discusses what the future holds for our company.

GO-TO-MARKET SLIDE

This section consists of one to two slides that talk about a company's growth trajectory over the next few years. For post-launch companies, you could call this a marketing, sales, or growth plan.

Y1/2/3 Goal/Kpi/Growth Tactics ✓

We used to list out a bunch of marketing or sales tactics and try and organize them intelligently. We saw mixed results with that strategy But, in the last year, I've landed on a great way to show go-to-market slides. I use a growth-curve visual and show goals, KPIs, and sales and marketing tactics for the next three years. It packs a fair amount of information onto a slide so that it doesn't look cluttered.

Compass Implications: The impact here is on growth tactics. Choose ones that align with your linchpin vector. More importantly, your linchpin vectors should shape all communication efforts beyond your investor pitch deck, including customer advertising, sales messaging, and corporate communications.

Bad Example: "*Here's our launch ad campaign that cost thousands of dollars. It talks about how fun it is to order from TastyDrone!*" If TastyDrone hired some hotshot agency to create a brand campaign that appealed to the emotional side of drone delivery, they made a mistake. Our communication priorities should be high speed and low cost. It would be a big missed opportunity if the campaign does not address those two factors.

Good Example: "In year one after launching in Austin, we aim to secure our first 50 restaurant partners, make our first 50,000 deliveries, and reach $500k in revenue. We plan to achieve that with founder-led direct sales outreach and local marketing efforts. In year two..." We love to include clear goals and KPIs on our go-to-market slides. The previous statement would have continued to outline the same elements for year two and year three after launch.

Bringing It Together: Go-to-Market Slide

Year One
• 1 City, 50 Restaurants, 50k Deliveries, $500k Revenue
• Tactics: Founder-led Direct Sales, Local Online/Offline Marketing

Year Two
• 2 Cities, 200 Restaurants, 300k Deliveries, $3M Revenue
• Tactics: Local Sales Team, Scale Docking Stations, Increase Local Marketing Efforts

Year Three
• 5 Cities, 500 Restaurants, 1M Deliveries, $10M Revenue
• Tactics: Scale Sales Teams, Upgrade Drone Batteries, State-wide Marketing Campaign

Original Go-To-Market Slide

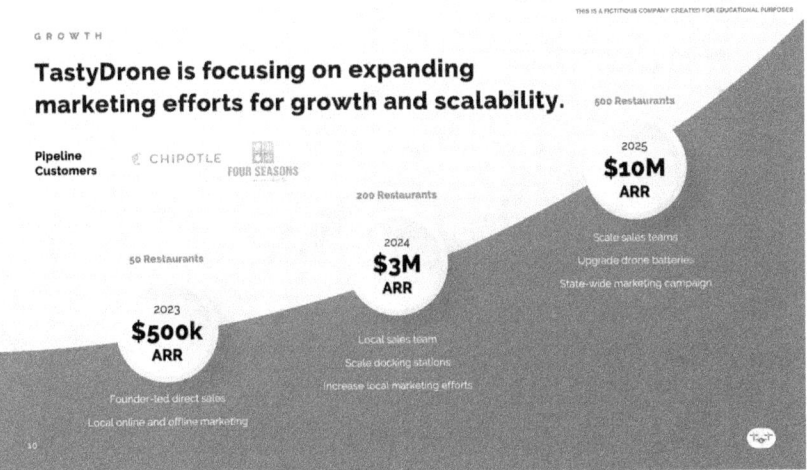

Updated Go-To-Market Slide

OPPORTUNITY SLIDE

Although we often bring up the market size on the first slide, we also like to have a dedicated, more detailed opportunity slide in the final third of our pitch decks. However, the opportunity slide isn't affected by your storyline compass because this slide is loaded with external observations and data.

Remember earlier when we said we needed to limit our revenue streams to the one that would bring in most of our revenue? The opportunity slide is a great place to put 1-3 additional new markets your startup could expand into. By the time you reach the back third of the deck, you've spent the first two-thirds highly focused on a single story. Now you can entice investors with the idea of market expansion.

Here's what we include on an opportunity slide.

Target Annual Opportunity (Not Impacted By Storyline Compass)

This is commonly defined as the total revenue your market or industry brings in over a year. We always aim to show opportunities that exceed $1 billion. Anything smaller than this and investors might not consider it large enough.

You can then break this down into segments. For example, total addressable market (largest), serviceable addressable market (smaller), and serviceable obtainable market (smallest). Investors often refer to these layers as TAM, SAM, and SOM.

First, I'll show you a top-down opportunity calculation.

For TastyDrone, the largest opportunity we could show would be the online restaurant delivery market and we would limit that to just the US. A quick Google search for "US online food delivery app market size" shows that the market is worth $22.4 billion in 2021. We can use that as a conservative TAM. We can now slice it based on the percentage of the US population living in Texas (9%) and end up with $2.02 billion. That's our SAM. Lastly, we would pick a small market share, such as 5%, and multiply our SAM by that to get our SOM of $101 million. This number says that if TastyDrone can capture 5% of all Texas deliveries, it will earn $101 million in revenue for that year.

Next, I'll show you a bottom-up opportunity calculation.

Investors see bottom-up calculations as the ideal way to calculate a company's revenue potential. For TastyDrone, I found that the average restaurant gets between 8 and 60 daily online orders. Our ultimate goal for TastyDrone is just five deliveries per restaurant per day. I'm okay if the rest are DoorDash or Uber Eats. We know we make a $10 per delivery fee, so that's $50 in revenue per day per restaurant and $18,250 per year per restaurant. Google tells me that are 43,000 restaurants in Texas and 661,000 in the US. So our total opportunity in Texas is $785 million, and $12 billion for the entire country.

Expansion Opportunities (Not Impacted By Storyline Compass)

This section of the pitch deck is where you can discuss additional revenue opportunities. If you have two or three additional ideas for revenue streams, list them here. Doing this helps you focus the rest of your presentation on the initial opportunity while showing investors that you have strong potential for future expansion into other markets or industries.

For TastyDrone, expansion into small parcel delivery and last-mile delivery in the US would be the focus of this section. For those, we'd just like the top-down TAM amount based on whatever we find on Google.

Original Opportunity Slide

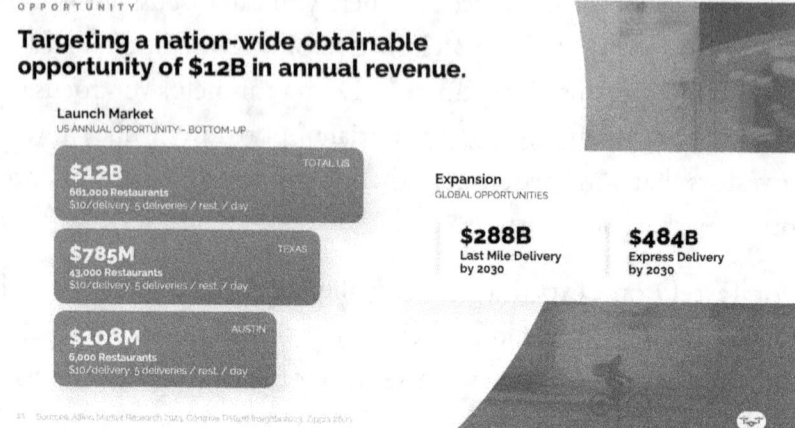

Targeting a nation-wide obtainable opportunity of $12B in annual revenue.

Launch Market
US ANNUAL OPPORTUNITY – BOTTOM-UP

$12B   TOTAL US
681,000 Restaurants
$10/delivery, 5 deliveries / rest. / day

$785M   TEXAS
43,000 Restaurants
$10/delivery, 5 deliveries / rest. / day

$108M   AUSTIN
6,000 Restaurants
$10/delivery, 5 deliveries / rest. / day

Expansion
GLOBAL OPPORTUNITIES

$288B
Last Mile Delivery
by 2030

$484B
Express Delivery
by 2030

THIS IS A FICTITIOUS COMPANY CREATED FOR EDUCATIONAL PURPOSES

Updated Opportunity Slide

VISION / ROADMAP SLIDE

This slide can be used as a detailed development roadmap or a big vision slide. If you've got many moving parts, then a roadmap works well. Otherwise, a vision slide works if you need to lay out a BHAG (big hairy audacious goal). Occasionally, we also create hybrid vision-roadmap slides.

The difference here is that a roadmap slide usually shows off fairly detailed quarterly or yearly business plans. On the other hand, a vision slide typically provides a high-level picture of what the business would look like in a decade if all goes according to plan and your startup changes the world. Founders articulate this vision as a big, bold statement. Examples are coming up!

The Big Vision ✓

For TastyDrone, I would lean toward a vision slide instead of a roadmap slide. If all goes according to plan, this business has the potential to fundamentally change the delivery game and make billions in the process.

Compass Implications: We use our storyline compass and linchpin vectors of high-speed, low-cost delivery to fuel the vision statement.

Bad Example: *"We're not just about delivering food; we want to give our customers a taste of the future."* The future is cool and all, but the fact that customers may feel like they're living in the future when they use our service doesn't align with our linchpin vector of accessibility.

Good Example: "*Making it possible to eat anything, anytime, anywhere.*" Using the word "eat" as the primary verb, we can stay within the food delivery space while still describing what the future could look like with TastyDrone.

"*Making it possible to get anything, anytime, anywhere.*" This is cool. By simply changing the word "eat" to "get," we broadened our business from food to anything. Anything encompasses small parcels, last-mile delivery, and other potential opportunities we have yet to identify.

Timeline Of Future Evolution ✓

Instead of a vision slide, the other option is a future timeline slide. This slide could take a couple of forms. In the case of TastyDrone, we've got two options: a geographic market launch plan (where we would show a map) or a detailed product development roadmap (a timeline of planned product features). I'll play out why both might be a good idea.

Compass Implications: If we at TastyDrone decide to show a map highlighting our key geographic target markets, we will indicate which ones they are, their rollout order, and the reason we chose each one. The storyline compass would not impact the order of that rollout.

On the other hand, if we included a detailed development timeline, we would align everything on that timeline to deliver a high-speed and low-cost product.

For our examples, we will focus on a product development time-line as the storyline compass impacts it more than the geographic market launch plan. I do love a nice map slide, though.

Bad Example: "*We want to make sure our orders are accurate. We're at 95% accuracy, but we can do better!*" If we're already at 95% order accuracy, we're good. Taking time to improve this may have diminishing returns. Either way, order accuracy doesn't align with our linchpin vector of accessibility.

Good Example: "*We're working on a new charging algorithm that will increase dispatch time by 25%.*" Focusing on improving our core solution is undoubtedly the best course of action for this early-stage company. When we reduce drone dispatch time, we increase the speed at which drones deliver orders. More orders mean more revenue potential and higher margins.

Bringing It Together: Vision / Roadmap Slide

(Instead of a product roadmap, I'll use a big vision slide for dramatic impact)

Vision
TastyDrone will make it possible to get anything, anytime, anywhere.

Long term, TastyDrone will expand to local retail and product delivery.

Local retailers
— Mom and pop retailers
— Local ecommerce

Big box retailers
— Targets, Walmarts
— White label

This is an example pitch deck for a fake company prepared for the **Startup Power Pitch Online Course** by STOSH PitchDecks.com

Original Vision / Roadmap Slide

THIS IS A FICTITIOUS COMPANY CREATED FOR EDUCATIONAL PURPOSES

LONG-TERM VISION

TastyDrone will make it possible to get anything, anytime, anywhere.

Updated Vision / Roadmap Slide

TEAM / ADVISORS SLIDE

Whenever a founder talks about themselves or their team, investors think, *"Why are these the right people for the job?"*

Studies have shown that the team behind a startup is one of the most significant contributors to success. It makes sense why investors have this top mind.

With teams, investors will first check for relevant experience. So, if the business were a biotechnology startup, we would need a leadership team with a proven track record in building and scaling biotechnology startups. They should also have a few PhDs on the team.

Team √

The team slide should always include the founders and key leadership. If you are a solo founder, include your advisers on the same slide as you to make it seem like a well-rounded team. Of the 140 pitch deck projects we've completed as of writing this book, only one or two were solo founders with no team or advisors. I don't think they raised either.

Teams are necessary, and building a successful startup takes a village, and investors expect to learn more about the village leaders on the team slide, even if it's just you and your co-founder.

In terms of the structure of the slide, we always recommend the following:

1. A maximum of five core team members
2. Professional-looking headshots for everyone
3. One or two-sentence bios for everyone. The first sentence includes years of relevant industry experience and companies. The second sentence includes notable career achievements.
4. A max of two relevant past company or client logos for everyone

Compass Implications: Based on the above, the two main things affected by the storyline compass are your two-sentence bios and the logos of relevant work experience. For TastyDrone, this could include experience with drones or restaurants, last-mile delivery, and experience at other startups in increasing delivery speed or reducing operational costs.

Bad Example: *"Jane Smith is our CEO and Co-Founder with over 10 years in global sales for Fortune 500 consumer packaged goods brands."* Jane is fantastic at sales and has excellent experience. But calling out enterprise-level CPG expertise might not send the right message as it has nothing to do with startups, restaurants, drones, or delivery. We can probably rewrite this expertise to seem more relevant.

"John Doe is our CTO and Co-Founder with over 15 years in technology operations at early-stage startups." Close, but "technology operations" is vague, so we might want to sharpen that to improve John's optics.

"Jane Smith is our CEO and Co-Founder and for the last 10 years she's been building and leading high-performance B2B sales teams for global brands." Here, we've done a few things better. First, we discuss how she built and led sales teams, which she'll need to do again for TastyDrone. Then, we've snuck in "high-performing" before we say "B2B" and "global brands" for some added credibility. Below this bio, we'll include logos for Jane's top two biggest or most relevant past employers.

"John Doe is our CTO and Co-Founder and for the last 15 years he's been a product lead and developer for early-stage startups and drone enthusiast." We've boosted the power by adding more specificity to John's past roles. Now, I'm assuming that John has drone experience. But, since it's only personal experience, I've called it out as such, labeling him an "enthusiast." We could elaborate on this if we included a second bio sentence on John.

Advisors ✓

Similar to the team slide, advisors and their experience must be relevant to your business and linchpin vector. Advisors should be selected based on what the business needs help with or the gaps they could fill in the leadership team. Regarding slide structure, I recommend:

1. A maximum of six advisors to a deck; investors count too
2. Professional or semi-professional headshots for everyone
3. What the advisor will advise on (e.g., Growth Advisor)
4. The advisor's current job title or last prominent position
5. A logo for the advisor's current company (two max each)

Compass Implications: First, ensure you're filling any gaps in the current leadership team. If you lack a chief marketing officer, find a marketing advisor. Next, ensure that advisor roles are relevant to your linchpin vector.

Bad Example: "Jane Smith from Rhombus Inc. is our advisor." We need to know a tiny bit more about Jane here. What type of advisor is she? What's her relationship with Rhombus Inc.? Why will she be an excellent advisor?

Good Example: "Jane Smith is our financial advisor and she is currently CFO and an Investor at Rhombus Inc." Now we're spelling out her expertise and how she will contribute to TastyDrone's success. Plus, we call out her relationship with Rhombus Inc. Not only is she CFO there, but she's also an investor, which elevates her value in the eyes of other investors. Also, since we're talking about being a low-cost competitor, her financial experience will also be there.

Bringing It Together: Team / Advisors Slide

(Have a look at the updated TastyDrone deck in the companion kit[1] for details.)

Original Team/Advisors Slide

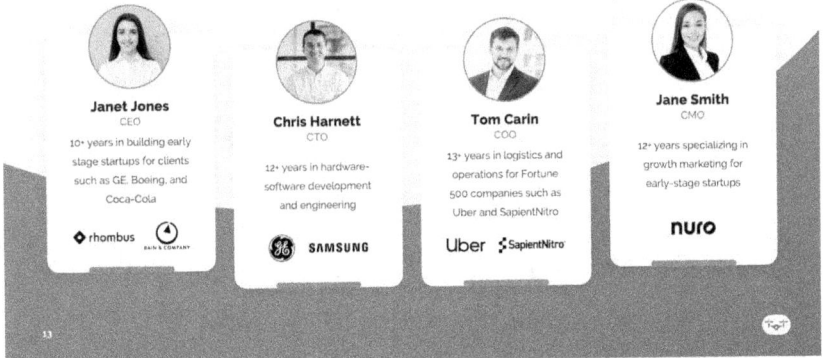

Updated Team/Advisors Slide

1. Download the companion kit at https://stry.pro/hgkit

FINANCIALS SLIDE

I've always recommended including some simple financial projections in your pitch deck. Investors know these will be wrong; it's just a matter of how wrong they'll be. Founders should always do their best to use real-world data for their forecasts. This data could come from their startup, customer surveys, third-party online reports, or other companies.

Financials should include the following:

1. A high-level five-year profit and loss statement
2. I recommend no more than two years of historical data
3. Label by year (e.g., 2023, 2024, etc.), not Year 1, Year 2, etc.
4. If there is past revenue, include a maximum of two years
5. Include one or two rows for relevant KPIs (e.g., # of customers)
6. Consolidated your expenses into three to five rows
7. Show a chart that visualizes revenue growth over time

Bringing It Together: Financials Slide

(I've updated these projections based on some research we conducted recently on financial projections. Check out our articles section on our website[1])

Aiming to hit $1 mil in revenue by Q2 2022 with rapid expansion afterwards.

	2021	2022	2023
Cities	1	1	7
Restaurants	100	900	3,000
Total Orders	18,800	604,800	2,016,500
Total Revenue	**$208,320**	**$7,499,520**	**$24,998,400**
Drones	200	1,100	6,000
Docking Stations	20	180	600
Drone Hardware	$280,000	$2,520,000	$8,400,000
Additional OpEx	$308,000	$2,772,000	$9,240,000
Total Expenses	**$588,000**	**$5,292,000**	**$17,640,000**
Operating Profit	**-$379,680**	**$2,207,520**	**$7,358,400**

TastyDrone

Original Financials Slide

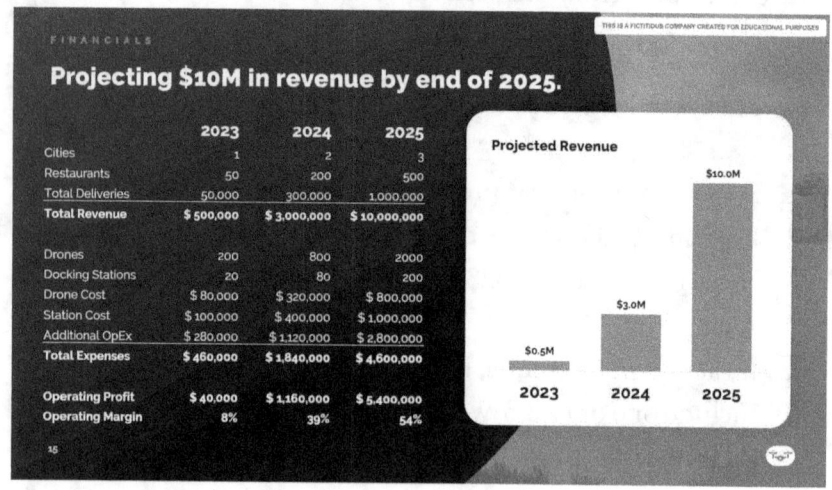

FINANCIALS

THIS IS A FICTITIOUS COMPANY CREATED FOR EDUCATIONAL PURPOSES

Projecting $10M in revenue by end of 2025.

	2023	2024	2025
Cities	1	2	3
Restaurants	50	200	500
Total Deliveries	50,000	300,000	1,000,000
Total Revenue	**$ 500,000**	**$ 3,000,000**	**$ 10,000,000**
Drones	200	800	2000
Docking Stations	20	80	200
Drone Cost	$ 80,000	$ 320,000	$ 800,000
Station Cost	$ 100,000	$ 400,000	$ 1,000,000
Additional OpEx	$ 280,000	$ 1,120,000	$ 2,800,000
Total Expenses	**$ 460,000**	**$ 1,840,000**	**$ 4,600,000**
Operating Profit	**$ 40,000**	**$ 1,160,000**	**$ 5,400,000**
Operating Margin	**8%**	**39%**	**54%**

Projected Revenue

Updated Financials Slide

---

1. storypitchdecks.com/articles

USE OF FUNDS SLIDE

This slide is where you tell investors what you need. How much should founders ask for? That's more of a question for a financial advisor, which I am not. However, our go-to response is, *"Ask for what you need to grow your company over the next 12-18 months."*

Lastly, we don't recommend putting your proposed company valuation or investment terms in your pitch deck. That's something better left for discussion. When you're having conversations, these elements can—and do—change from investor to investor.

How You'll Spend It ✓

The main element on this slide affected by the storyline compass is how you'll spend investor funds. How a business plan on using investor proceeds is quite important, so I will dedicate a small section to explaining this in more detail right now.

———

ALIGNING YOUR USE OF FUNDS WITH YOUR LINCHPIN VECTOR

Typically, founders can boil down all use of funds resulting from a capital raise can be boiled down into three buckets:

1. _Product or Services_ - Money spent on improving, upgrading, overhauling, or building something that will benefit a startup's core offering.
2. _Marketing and Sales_ - Money spent on awareness-driving or brand-building initiatives to acquire new customers.
3. _General and Administrative_ - Money spent on general operations and overhead that keeps the lights on.

You may be wondering, _"What about staffing?"_ Rolling staffing budgets into each category mentioned above is the best way to display this information. For example, if you need to hire ten developers, move their salaries into products or services. If you need to hire a head of marketing and two sales leads, include their salaries in the marketing and sales bucket. Last, if you need to pay leaders who operate across the entire business, move their wages into the general and administrative category. If you need office space, data services, software subscriptions, or other operational components, founders should also roll those costs into the general and administrative category.

If you need help planning how to use investor proceeds, here are a few ideas on how to structure them. The numbers presented here are guidelines, and there are exceptions to each.

USE OF FUNDS FOR EFFICACY

Product - Continual spending on product improvements is vital to ensure a startup keeps or gains a competitive edge.

Marketing/Sales - Businesses that operate in an efficacy space will need to ensure that they have concrete evidence of the effectiveness of their solutions in the form of data. They can then use that data in their marketing and sales initiatives to increase customer acquisition.

General/Admin - At the overarching level, founders might incur additional expenses to continue providing the most effective solution in the market.

Example Allocations For Efficacy

Seed - B2C, B2B

- Product - 40%, 60%

- Marketing/Sales - 40%, 30%

- General/Admin - 20%, 10%

Series-A - B2C, B2B

- Product - 30%, 40%

- Marketing/Sales - 60%, 40%

- General/Admin - 10%, 20%

USE OF FUNDS FOR ACCESSIBILITY

Product - When accessibility is a linchpin vector, ensuring that startup's core solution becomes increasingly easy to access is vital.

Marketing/Sales - For businesses operating with accessibility as a linchpin vector, communicating their core offerings and the advantages of hiring them for accessibility is critical.

General/Admin - Companies here should consider investing more in their operations, customer service, and support. This approach ensures they meet the criteria associated with accessibility and achieve higher levels of customer satisfaction.

Example Allocations For Accessibility

Seed - B2C, B2B

- Product - 40%, 60%

- Marketing/Sales - 30%, 25%

- General/Admin - 30%, 15%

Series-A - B2C, B2B

- Product - 30%, 40%

- Marketing/Sales - 50%, 35%

- General/Admin - 20%, 25%

USE OF FUNDS FOR ENJOYMENT

Product - Companies that prioritize the enjoyment of their product need to allocate a sufficient budget to ensure that the product remains enjoyable and continues to surprise and delight their customers.

Marketing/Sales - Founders must spend money to ensure potential customers know how enjoyable a startup's experience is.

General/Admin - To ensure that the usage of the product remains enjoyable, it is often necessary to invest in business and operational activities.

Example Allocations for Enjoyment

Seed - B2C, B2B

• Product - 40%, 40%

• Marketing/Sales - 40%, 25%

• General/Admin - 20%, 30%

Series A - B2C, B2B

• Product - 30%, 40%

• Marketing/Sales - 50%, 35%

• General/Admin - 20%, 35%

USE OF FUNDS FOR CONNECTION

Product - Founders of a startup that sells physical products mainly incur expenses here when the product is in initial development. Further product expenditures usually come in the form of purchasing inventory.

Marketing/Sales - Companies that require an emotional connection to succeed in their category should allocate as much of their budget as possible to marketing, branding, and sales.

General/Admin - Founders should minimize overhead and operational costs for companies that require an emotional connection as much as possible so they can spend money on product and marketing.

I omitted B2B companies below as it's likely that the sort of businesses would not have a linchpin vector of emotional connection.

Example Allocations for Connection

Seed - B2C

• Product - 30%

• Marketing/Sales - 60%

• General/Admin - 10%

Series A - B2C

• Product - 20%

• Marketing/Sales - 70%

• General/Admin - 10%

———

Alrighty! That wraps up my little side section on the use of funds and linchpin vectors. Now, let's move on to the final slide in your deck.

Bringing It Together: Use Of Funds Slide

How Much You're Raising
$1 Million

How You'll Spend It
• Product - 50%
• Marketing/Sales - 30%
• General/Admin - 20%

Over How Long

18 Months of Operational Runway

What Will It Help Achieve
- Make enough drones and stations to launch
- Boost sales efforts with restaurant owners
- Consumer marketing launch in Austin, TX

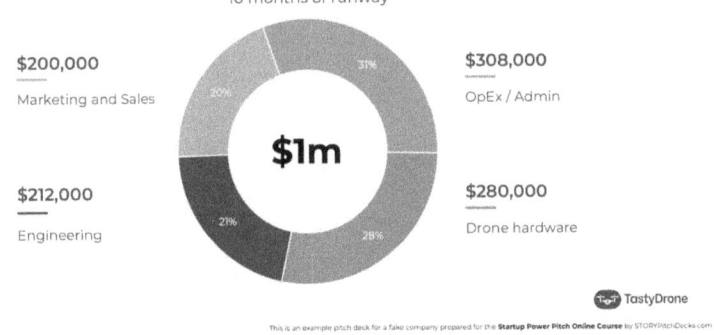

Original Use of Funds Slide

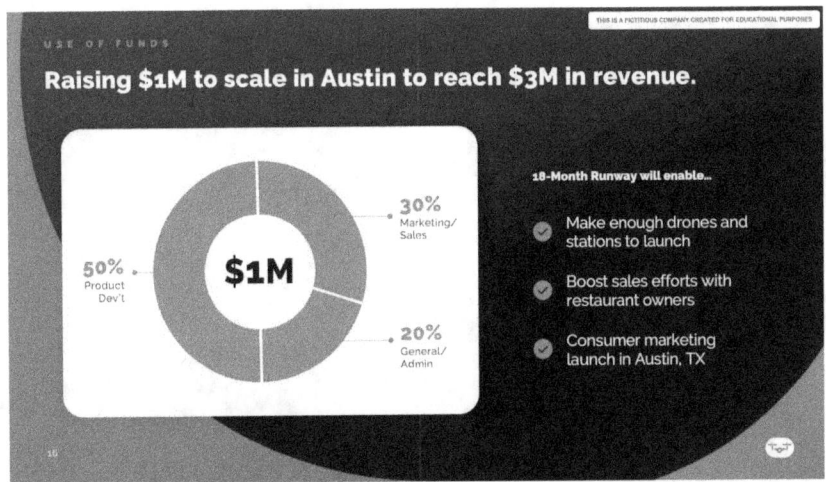

Updated Use of Funds Slide

WHY NOW SLIDE

I look at an entire pitch deck as making a case for "Why now." I also like to use the last slide in the deck to recap the three things we want investors to remember. After 15 slides of content, it's easy for messaging to get lost in the specifics. So, these three things should restate the most compelling reasons for investors to back your company. Another way to approach this is to summarize the three most important takeaways from the pitch deck in less than a sentence each.

Why Is Now The Best Time ✓

Why do investors care about timing? Venture capitalist analysts have conducted studies showing that timing is the single most significant factor contributing to a startup's success next to the team. If you Google "timing startup success study," you'll find many articles and videos on this topic.

Explaining "Why now" requires reflection on factors like your region's current macroeconomic conditions, industry-specific conditions, and microeconomics affecting your startup. You should also consider the regulatory environment, investor sentiment, and the state of critical technology impacting your startup.

Compass Implications: Think back to your storyline compass. This tool gives you a clear picture of the benefits your company provides relative to the direct and indirect competition within your category. You can combine this with the aforementioned factors (e.g., macro and micro economic conditions) to create some good "Why now" bullet points.

Bad Example: "America's only drone delivery service." We avoid using statements like "the first" or "the world's only" because they are often untrue. If the statement is true, it may suggest that this is the first time anyone else has seen this as a lucrative opportunity, which is not a positive point for investors.

<u>*Good Example:*</u> *"Early-mover opportunity to disrupt an unprofitable industry."* For TastyDrone, this is compelling in two ways. First, the word 'early' implies that this market is in the early stages of development and will likely grow to be a massive industry within a few years; and we are reminding the investors that the current multi-billion dollar takeout delivery industry is wildly and profitable and not sustainable)

Bringing It Together: Why Now Slide

Why Is Now The Best Time
Drone and AI technologies have reached a tipping point and the race for this delivery modality is on.

What 3 Things The Investor Should Remember
1. Patent-pending hardware and software
2. Successful pilots program in Austin, TX
3. LOIs from top global and local brands

TastyDrone

JOIN US AS WE FINALLY GET FOOD DELIVERY PROFITABLE.

- COVID has fast-tracked at-home food delivery
- Human labor is unscalable and not the way forward
- TastyDrone's scalable drone tech cracks the profitability code

Janet Jones
CEO
1-234-567-8910
janet@tastydrone.com

Original Why Now Slide

Updated Why Now Slide

WRAPPING UP FUTURE STATE

There we go! We've just gone through all 42 elements of a 15-slide pitch deck, showing you how to elevate the strength of your story to a line to your company's primary solution benefit.

In our last section, we'll look at how to eliminate content from your pitch deck that is unnecessary, redundant, or distracting from your core message.

PART TWO RECAP
ELEVATE YOUR STRENGTHS

The Storyline Compass

A quadrant-based tool where competitors are plotted across four vectors using a radar chart: Efficacy, Enjoyment, Accessibility, and Connection.

These four vectors represent every possible benefit a company could provide its customers and helps visualize how each is positioned in a given category or industry.

Creating a Storyline Compass

1. Select 3-5 direct and indirect competitors to compare
2. Subjectively rate each startup on a scale of one to ten for each of the four vectors. For example, *"How effective is company A at solving their customer's problem compared to others?"*
3. Visualize your data table using a radar chart in whatever spreadsheet tool you prefer

Using the Storyline Compass

Once completed, determine your linchpin vector (the primary vector you're going to compete on) and align every element in your pitch deck to that.

-PART THREE-
ELIMINATE THE FLUFF

CHAPTER 7

ELIMINATING FLUFF IN YOUR PITCH

FLUFF IS the stuff in your pitch deck that blurs your message. It distracts the audience from what's important. I discussed how to focus your pitch's message in the second part of this book. This third and final part will show you how to trim the fat in your pitch deck so that your focused message stays loud and clear.

As a founder, you're in the weeds. You are knee-deep in building a business and all of the beautiful complexity that comes with it. While this sort of heads-down immersion is necessary, founders often need to take a step back and try and look at the big picture when building their pitch deck.

However, stepping back is much easier said than done. Everything in this book is about helping founders take that step back to see the forest through the trees.

Founders tend to include way too much information in their pitch deck. It's not about putting *everything* in there, though. It's about just having *the right things* and nothing else. Investors do not need to understand your business at the same detailed level that you do as a founder. Realistically, founders only have a few minutes with investors to tell their stories in the most compelling way possible. Conveying all possible information about your business to investors in that timeframe is physically impossible. So, the task becomes more about sharing enough information so investors understand what you're doing, why you are doing it, why it's a good investment, and nothing more.

Say it with me: *a great pitch deck conveys the right information and nothing more.* Anything that isn't "the right information" is fluff, and pitch decks contain fluff in many shapes and sizes. In this section, I'll explain the various forms of fluff commonly found in pitch decks.

WHAT TO DO WITH FLUFF

In just a second, I'll go through ways to identify fluff. But what do you do with fluff once you've identified it? Do you just delete it? Put it in a colossal appendix? Burn it with fire?

There are three options for dealing with fluff:

1. Put it in an appendix after your last slide in the pitch deck
2. Put it in a "parking lot" document containing all your cut content
3. Put it in the main pitch deck and elevate its importance

Put It In An Appendix

There's a good chance that you'll come across some slides or content that you've created that aren't necessary for your main pitch but are essential for investor discussions after you've finished your pitch.

This case is when a pitch deck appendix is the most useful. Appendix slides aren't usually presented and always come after the last slide in your main pitch. Instead, appendix slides are discussion aides for specific topics in your pitch. Appendix slides also help answer common investor questions. However, if investors always ask the same question, founders should consider adding a slide to answer it in their pitch before it's asked.

How many slides should your appendix be?

Keep it to only a few slides. It's okay if each is a standalone slide that simply sheds more light on a topic within your pitch deck and doesn't necessarily tell a sequential story. An example appendix could include more details on your competitors, additional charts highlighting your current customer base, or further information on how your technology works.

Because investors are all unique, each will have their own unique lens for viewing your business. In the early stages of pitching, deciding which slides to include in an appendix is a guess. By pitching investors, some slides will feel more important than others as you talk them through. Scrutinize each slide as you pitch to investors and determine whether or not each is working as hard as it can or if it's fluff.

. . .

Put It in A Parking Lot

I don't recommend deleting or overwriting content or slides once founders have created them. You might need them at some point. You put the effort and the thinking into them, so don't waste them.

That's where a parking lot document or folder comes in handy. A parking lot is a presentation document containing slides or content you've cut. Sometimes, I'll put all the old slides I didn't use into the back of the pitch deck and hide them so they aren't presented or exported.

Parking lots don't have a maximum length, so go nuts. If you remove a slide or some slide content, simply cut it from your latest and greatest version of your pitch deck and paste it into your parking lot.

Be sure to keep your parking lot somewhat organized. For instance, you could create sections correlating to your primary pitch deck, such as a problem or solution slide. Or, you could organize by the type of content, such as explainer graphics, data charts, or research you conducted.

Put It in Your Main Pitch Deck

Getting to a great pitch deck is a long and winding process for most. Without carefully listening and considering investor feedback, founders can go crazy trying to please everyone, including themselves. It's okay to modify your pitch each time you present. Often, founders will cut a slide thinking it's fluff, only to update it and add them back into their deck after a few more pitches.

It's not fluff if you cut something only to be asked questions about it during your next investor pitch. In this case, how you presented the information was probably where the challenge was.

CHAPTER 8
ELIMINATING GENERAL FLUFF

IN THIS SECTION, I'll cover fluff that could affect your entire pitch deck. The types of fluff that fall into this category are broad and usually result from not knowing what to cut or how to cut it.

Too Many Slides for Your Round

The most common issue with startups is having too many or too few slides. We at STORY Pitch Decks gathered 100 publicly-available pitch decks that raised capital and divided them up based on round. We then calculated the average slide count for each round, and here's what we found:

- Pre-seed: 12 - 15 slides
- Seed: 15 - 17 slides
- Series-A: 17 - 19 slides
- Series-B or higher: 20 - 25 slides

These slide counts are what I use for my clients as well. Why the change in presentation lengths? More mature companies have more content to cover, like product-market fit data, financial performance, and customer metrics. For even later-stage companies, the focus shifts to more details around growth strategy and expansion plans.

Taking Too Long to Get to The Point

I'll get specific here. Taking too long to reach the point usually means having too many slides in your upfront or the number of slides it takes to get to your solution slide. These slides are usually your title, trend, problem, and solution slides.

Investors want you to dive in as fast as possible. What your company does is what interests them. But, when founders have too many slides before their solution slide, they take too long to reach the point investors care about most.

Here's a reference for your upfront section:

Title - Only have one title slide.

Trend - Aim for one slide. Only another slide here if it's necessary to educate your investors on what you're doing.

Problem - Stick to a single slide. Add another slide here only if it's necessary to educate your investors on what you're doing.

Solution - Only have one solution slide.

TOTAL BEFORE SOLUTION: 3-4 slides

Ideally, aim for three, only adding one more if necessary.

If you need to add another upfront slide, only do so to provide more context. Investors enjoy learning new things, and another slide that includes more complex or knowledge-intense macro trends within an industry could be a good thing.

But most decks don't need more than one trend and one problem slide. Adding more than this slide dilutes your message about the actual problem. Also, you would need to solve the problems on both slides with a single solution slide.

If your company has two target audiences, like in the case of marketplaces, founders should keep these problems on a single slide. To do this, split your problem slide in half, with half of the slide talking about problems for one audience and the other half talking about the issues for a different audience.

Too Much Text on Each Slide

This problem is common, and we always hear the same thing from founders. They'll say, "There's no way you can cut this text down anymore. Everything in it is important!" Guess what? You can almost always find a way to say the same thing with fewer words. Being economical with your words is a skill that founders should practice, and there's no better place than with your pitch deck.

I'll give you a few examples.

Original Text (141 characters, 17 words):

> *Rhombus is an accounting automation software that provides real-time, asynchronous, cloud-based bookkeeping for small and medium enterprises.*

Why it's bad: We'd never include long-form sentences or paragraphs on a slide. It's not necessary. While the writer packed this sentence with specifics, it uses too many words to do so.

Edited Text (39 characters, five words):

> *Rhombus: Automated bookkeeping for SMEs*

Why it's better: Words like "automated" are easy to understand and imply ideas like real-time and asynchronous, which are similar in meaning. We have also introduced a common acronym for small and medium enterprises ("SMEs") to eliminate more words.

Here's another example, this time for TastyDrone.

Original Text (200 characters, 28 words)

> *TastyDrone uses a proprietary artificial intelligence stack to pilot tens of thousands of drones simultaneously while plotting the most efficient flight patterns to ensure timely delivery of payloads.*

Why it's bad: Founders should avoid sentences that are longer than ten to twelve words in presentations. Multiple studies have shown that sentences that are longer than ten words have diminishing returns in the form of lower comprehension and memory recall rates. There are also a lot of redundant words here.

Edited Text (135 characters, 16 words):

TastyDrone's autonomous piloting engine:

- *100% proprietary, patent-pending*

- *Pilots 50,000+ drones at once*

- *Optimizes flights in real-time*

Why it's better: Splitting long sentences into short bullets enables audiences to scan each point for essential information quickly. These bullets also provide reminders to the presenter of what their talking points should be. We've also squeezed in more specifics by saying "patent pending" and mentioning the number of drones the software can pilot simultaneously.

If you need a rule to follow, aim for full-sentence headlines at the top of each slide that are twelve words or less, and keep the total word count for each slide between 20 and 50 words. Sometimes you'll need to go higher but force yourself to get out that editing machete and slash your way to clear and brief slides.

Too Many Fancy Words

We aim for a ninth-grade reading level in pitch decks, which means keeping words simple, avoiding too much industry jargon, and steering clear of lesser-known acronyms.

Long, complex sentences don't make you seem more intelligent or competent. Instead, the opposite is true. Studies have shown that as the amount of jargon in a body of text increases, the less likely it is that audiences will find that text trustworthy. Search for "jargon trustworthy article study" and read the first couple of results if you'd like to dive deeper.

Jargon levels can change based on the types of investors you're presenting to. Technical investors will understand technical terminology; the same goes for other subject matter experts. But everyone understands straightforward language, regardless of professional or academic background.

Here are a couple of examples from PlainLanguage.gov:

INSTEAD OF SAYING:

Riverine avifauna

SAY:

River birds

INSTEAD OF SAYING:

Involuntarily undomiciled

SAY:

Homeless

INSTEAD OF SAYING:

The patient is being given positive-pressure ventilatory support.

SAY:

The patient is on a respirator.

INSTEAD OF SAYING:

Most refractory coatings to date exhibit a lack of reliability when subject to the impingement of entrained particulate matter in the propellant stream under extended firing durations.

SAY:

The exhaust gas eventually damages the coating of most existing ceramics.

Need more help with brevity? Here are a few free tools to help out:

- grammarly.com
- hemingwayapp.com
- powerthesaurus.org
- onelook.com/reverse-dictionary.shtml

Too Many Explainer Graphics

Plenty of fluff exists in infographics or explainer visuals. While graphics can be incredibly useful in communicating complex topics with only a few words, it's easy to overdo it and make visuals or graphics too complicated.

We recommend a maximum of two to three explainer graphics per pitch deck, and founders shouldn't have more than a single explainer visual per idea. If you use two different visuals to explain the same idea, you've now made things more complicated, not less. Just use one graphic to present one idea as clearly as possible.

When we include too many explainer graphics in their pitch, they get mixed up in our audience's minds. As a result, when investors think back to a pitch with too many visuals, they might find it challenging to recall the core message. This issue is especially prevalent for pitch decks with visuals that are too similar. For instance, if you need to explain two different processes, don't use similar graphics to explain each process. Instead, make each different enough so investors can tell at a glance that they're talking about two distinct ideas.

Only use similar graphics when you're explaining similar ideas. For instance, if you want to explain processes for two types of users, use similar process graphics for each user group. You could even combine these two graphics onto one slide to compare them side-by-side.

Here are three examples to demonstrate this point.

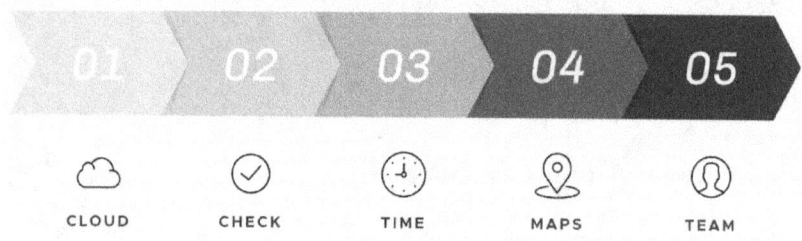

Explainer Graphic A

Explainer Graphic B

Explainer Graphic C

At first glance, graphics A and B look like they are saying the same thing because they're similar in layout and structure. Each has five steps, and both go left to right. Each step also has text under a few icons. But, when you look more closely, you can see that the order of each is different.

Meanwhile, graphic C visually looks like it's a different process. It uses circles instead of boxes and has four steps instead of five. While this process is also left-to-right and linear, it's different enough visually that investors would assume it's talking about something different.

Carefully consider all of the explainer graphics in your deck. If each illustration isn't adding to the overall strength of your story, it's most likely distracting from it.

Too Much Data

Including data in your pitch deck is a must. Exemplary data from the right source included on the right slide can significantly strengthen your story's credibility.

However, sometimes it can turn into a dumpster fire. The problem begins when founders throw too much data at a given slide or idea. The result is a dilution of the overall impact of the slide. More data does not equal more credibility. Using just the right data and nothing else should be the goal.

Here's a quick reference for the slides that usually have data points:

Trend - We regularly include some type of data on the trend slide. I would recommend limiting it to no more than three data points or statistics and one excellent chart.

Problem - We will occasionally include data for each pain point on a problem slide. However, I've noticed that problem slides can become too cluttered if you show one data point for each statement. If we have three problem statements, each with a data point, we would have six total pieces of content for the problem slide. Instead, I recommend using three short problem statements with a single statistic to emphasize all three points.

Solution - We usually don't include any data on a solution slide. The only exception is when the data point explains how a solution is superior to other alternatives. For instance, *"200% faster results"* would work fine if it was the only data point on the slide.

Traction - It's easy to throw a lot of data points at the traction slide. I recommend limiting it to six data points and one chart showing momentum; usually revenue, transaction volume, or customer growth.

Competition - Certain competition slides, such as the four-box or the magic quadrant, don't require statistics or data points. However, suppose you include a feature function grid comparing multiple companies across several attributes. In that case, it's a perfect opportunity to have a row that shows the same data point for each. For example, in the case of TastyDrone, we could compare average delivery times and fees across each competitor and ourselves.

Opportunity - The opportunity slide is entirely data-driven. I recommend splitting this slide into the launch or initial opportunity and the expansion opportunities. The launch opportunity will have one big data point (usually in billions of dollars) and a few more minor data points (usually billions or hundreds of millions of dollars). I recommend limiting the expansion opportunities to three, each with a data point in billions of dollars.

Now that you know the general limits for data points in a pitch deck, how do you decide which are the best ones to include? I've got another reference list for that:

Relevance - How relevant is the data point to the idea you're trying to articulate? Founders can ensure data points are relevant by aligning them with each slide's core concept. For instance, if the message you want to communicate is that giraffes have the longest necks relative to their height, simply stating that the average neck length of a female giraffe is seven feet wouldn't be enough. Instead, a more relevant statistic would be the neck-to-body ratio of a giraffe compared to other long-necked animals. Always make sure your data speaks to the main point of the slide it's on.

Recency - How recent was the data collected? Check whether the publisher gathered data in the last two years to ensure it is current. However, if you have difficulty finding data about something niche, it might be necessary to go back a bit further. In this case, the number one thing to consider is whether or not a significant macroeconomic event happened between now and when they conducted the study. I'm looking at you, COVID-19.

Credibility - Was the data gathered collected by a credible source? Source credibility is a subjective topic. Founders can consider data trustworthy if the publisher has a good reputation. Investors consider companies like Accenture, McKinsey, Deloitte, Bloomberg, Harvard Business Review, Forbes, or the Wall Street Journal credible because they're well-known. If you need more robust data, you can check out industry-centric research firms like IBISWorld, Forrester, and eMarketer. Additionally, many academic institutions provide research services that are worth exploring. Just be sure to cite your sources on each slide that contains data.

Methodology - Was the data collected correctly from the right place? The sample size is the main thing founders should pay attention to here. Without going too deep into the math of statistics, the sample size is the number of data points used to arrive at a specific statistic. The larger the sample size, the more accurate a data set is. Let's say we ask three people what their favorite drink is. Two say Coca-Cola, and one says Kombucha. Based on this sample size of three (n=3), our statistic would be "One in three people like kombucha, and kombucha is the second most popular drink." However, our sample size is too small to make a statistically significant conclusion. Instead, if we asked a few thousand people from all age ranges and genders with even distribution across the US, we would have a much more robust sample size. The conclusions drawn from that data set would be much more reliable.

Example time! We found the following statistic and want to include it on our trend slide:

Accountants handle 100-200 emails daily, about 24 hours each week.

The point we're trying to articulate with this data is that accountants spend too much time on administrative tasks and not enough time on high-level, critical thinking.

Now, let's run this stat through our checklist.

Relevance - Since we're trying to demonstrate that accountants spend too much time on administrative tasks, and email is considered an administrative task, the relevance here is high. But, if we wanted to have a more relevant stat, we should try to find a study that groups administrative tasks into one bucket instead of looking at email only. An ideal stat would look like this:

Accountants spend 3-4 hours each day on administrative tasks. A complimentary stat would look like this: *95% of accountants want more time for critical thinking.*

Recency - Let's assume the current year is 2023. The original stat about accountants is from 2015 and is eight years old. That's too old to include in a deck made in 2023, especially when we consider the effect COVID-19 had on the workplace. Ideally, we find a statistic from 2021 or 2022 to make this as recent as possible.

Credibility - From what I can tell, this statistic came from a report conducted by Karbon Magazine. However, when I dug around the web to find the original study, I couldn't find it anywhere. Oddly, Karbon is the only place this study mentioned, a blog site owned by Quickbooks accounting software. Because I couldn't track down the original research, this raises a red flag, telling me that the data might not be that reliable.

Methodology - Since I couldn't find the original source, I could not determine the methodology behind it. Report writers usually include a section that tells readers when they collected the data, the sample size, and the sample demographics. For example, let's assume the 100-200 emails per day stat came from a study of 300 independent accounting consultants in the US and Canada. While 300 is a good sample size for this smaller audience, the study only focused on independent accounting consultants. This report might not be relevant if we wanted to know how accountants at large companies spent their day.

Don't Forget To Cite Your Sources

The last point I'll make about including data in your pitch deck is to cite your sources. I mentioned it earlier, but whenever you use a data point, a chart, or a statistic on a slide, be sure to include a small footer that sites the source of that data point, chart, or statistic like this:

Source: Pew Research, 2022 (n=300)

We usually include the name of the source, the year it was published, and the sample size (articulated here by n=300). We could also add the survey's panel demographics next to the sample size and say *"n=300 independent accountants,"* for example.

CHAPTER 9
ELIMINATING SLIDE-SPECIFIC FLUFF

To wrap up this book, I will cover fluff at the slide level. This sort of fluff is small and detail-oriented. But beauty is always in the details, and soon you'll learn how to find and eliminate fluff as it appears in most pitch deck slides.

More Than One Problem Slide - As mentioned previously, sticking with one problem slide is best. Having multiple problem slides can convey a lack of focus on your part to investors.

If you currently have several problem slides, go through an editing exercise where you list out every single problem that your solution solves for each audience that it solves it. Next, rank each for relevance according to the storyline compass and your linchpin vector. If you have one audience that will use your solution, include a maximum of three problem statements for that audience. If you have two audiences, include a maximum of two problem statements for each audience for a total of four problem statements. If you have three audiences, eliminate one and focus on your two most important ones.

Overcomplicated Problem - An over-complicated problem comes from a need for more understanding of that problem. The best way to simplify an over-complicated problem is to use the storyline compass and align your problem to your linchpin vector.

More Than One Solution Slide - As a reminder, I only recommend having one solution slide. The solution slide typically contains a few benefit statements, each addressing a problem statement from the previous slide. Occasionally, founders could also include some features from your product or service. I would also avoid including a solution slide and a value proposition slide. They're the same thing, so make one great one and lose the other.

Overcomplicated Solution - If you have an over-complicated problem, you will have an over-complicated solution. By streamlining your problem slide down to the essential information, you can use your problem slide as a template to write the solution slide.

As mentioned, if you invert the problem statements, you will have benefits statements. Here's what I mean:

Problems:

- A slow, manual process
- Choice overload
- Inconsistent output quality

Inverted Problems (Benefits):

- Fast, automated workflow
- Streamlined decision-making
- 99.9% consistent output

See how each statement is like two sides of the same coin? You can also do this in reverse by inverting benefit statements into problem statements. It's a great technique to ensure you've aligned your messaging and eliminated fluff.

More Than Three Product/How It Works Slides - Product slides, or how it works slides, explain the details of your solution. For early-stage decks, it's easy to go overboard and include too many product detail slides. We usually have a minimum of one product slide, occasionally up to two product slides, and rarely up to three. Founders should avoid four.

The best way to show off a product using only one product slide is to include a video walk-through without any audio. The presenter can then describe what's happening in the video to the investor as it's happening. Effectively, this becomes a live demo using a pre-recorded video.

Overcomplicated Revenue Model - Sometimes, pricing your product or services is complicated. Often, startups have multiple pricing tiers, packages, add-ons, volume discounts, and more. Each one of these creates many layers of complexity.

While the reality may be complex, in the world of pitch decks, it's all about simplicity. Following the rule of threes, limit the number of products and prices to three. For instance, your primary revenue stream would have one price; if you have any additional add-ons, those would be your other two.

If you still need to simplify it, consider using a price range. For example, "Our basic plan ranges from $5 - $10 per month depending on features." In the case of B2B businesses, this is a perfect opportunity to mention your average contract value. Usually abbreviated as ACV, this metric is the average revenue a new customer account brings to the business over a year.

More Than One Competition Slide - We rarely include more than one competition slide. The main thing with simplifying here is choosing the right visual to show. We've researched this topic, and we have found that there are four common ways to illustrate a competitive landscape in a pitch deck. Pick one and make it as compelling as possible. Here they are:

Four Box / Magic Quadrant - This visual is one of the most common we see, and you're likely familiar with it. It uses an X-Y axis to compare all companies within a given industry across the two axes. Usually, your startup is in the upper-right-hand corner looking all high and mighty. Each axis is a fantastic place to bring back your linchpin vectors.

Feature-Function Grid - This table-based visual is also very common. The table's top row shows your startup alongside a handful of competitors. Below this top row are subsequent rows highlighting specific attributes across each company in the table. Typically, founders only bring attention to particular features as the main point of comparison. However, using comparison attributes that go beyond features and look at the company overall is the best way to use the feature-function grid.

Petal Chart - A petal chart looks like a Venn diagram. Founders should use this visual when their startup combines elements common to two or more different types of companies in their startup's industry.

Replace / Augment / Compliment - We came up with this one, and it's super useful for companies that don't fit into any of the buckets mentioned above. It consists of three columns representing three groups of competitors. The first column consists of competitors your product replaces (e.g., TastyDrone would *replace* DoorDash for consumers). The second column mentions competitors that you augment or improve (e.g., TastyDrone would *augment* or improve in-house delivery drivers for restaurants). The final column lists competitors your business *compliments* or sits alongside (e.g., TastyDrone compliments big brands like Starbucks and Chipotle). To finish the graphic, you would place your startup's logo above the table columns with an arrow extending from your logo across all three columns.

More Than Two Marketing/Sales Slides - We touched on the go-to-market slide earlier in the "Elevate" section of this book, but we usually only include one marketing and sales slide: the go-to-market or growth slide. Mature companies might need one slide dedicated to their marketing and one to sales.

Paragraph-long Team Bios - In early-stage pitch decks, the team is critical. But that doesn't mean each founder gets a full-page biography in your deck. Instead, stick to just one or two sentences for each team member. Earlier in this book, I covered what the structure of those sentences should look like.

In addition to the formulas for those two sentences, I recommend keeping personal stuff like where you live, your hobbies, and other things off this slide to keep it brief.

Boom! There we go. General fluff, covered. Slide-specific fluff, sorted. I'll give you one more tip on handling investor feedback as you begin presenting your deck.

Handling Investor Feedback: Look for The Overlap

Unfortunately, like everything else in Startup World, there is no hard-and-fast set of rules for founders to decide what to cut or include in their pitch. Yes, this book has some good guidelines, but that's all they are.

The reality is that pitch decks are highly subjective.

Some of the most successful startups in history had their subpar pitch deck turned down dozens of times before landing an investor. Every investor will have an opinion on what you should and shouldn't do with your pitch deck.

Your job is to prepare a deck that satisfies 80 to 90% of what investors are looking for. They will have questions. They will have feedback. They will overflow with suggested changes for your pitch deck.

When pitching to investors, I advise founders to look for overlaps in their feedback. If, for example, each investor has five pieces of feedback and you pitch to ten investors, you'll end up with 50 points of feedback. While much of that feedback will be unique to each investor, patterns will emerge. Usually, around 10% to 20% of all feedback a founder receives will be the same across every investor.

That overlap is what you need to look for.

So, out of 50 points of feedback, founders may see that five points are similar across most investors. These points are what a founder should heavily consider addressing when revising their pitch. As for the remaining feedback, founders could de-prioritize them as fixing minor issues will likely have a limited impact on how compelling the story is.

If your pitch deck is an 8 out of 10 before showing it to investors, and then you address those major feedback points, you'll likely be a 9.5 out of 10 after.

Notice how I didn't say a perfect ten there? Your pitch deck will never be perfect. Perfect is unattainable by definition. It's a theoretical state, and you'll never be able to reach it physically. Again, think of your pitch as being "always in beta," and you'll have a great mindset in place.

ELIMINATE THE FLUFF

General Fluff Elimination Checklist

- Aim for 15-20 slides max. depending on your round
- Only have 3-4 slides before the solution slide
- Keep slides under 50 words total incl. <10-word headlines
- Limit jargon and acronyms, aim for 9th-grade reading level
- Use fewer than 3 explainer graphics, one per idea
- Remove all data that isn't pertinent to the slide's point

How many slides should my pitch have? *Fewer slides are always preferred.*

Title: 1 (max. 3 logos or 1 testimonial)

Trend: 1 (2 slides for complex industries only)

Problem: 1 (max. 3 sub-problems)

Solution: 1 (benefits are inverse of sub-problems)

Product: 1-3 (max. 3-4 key features per product)

Model: 1 (max. 3 pricing groups)

Competition: 1 (max. 1 competitive visual)

Growth: 1 (2 slides for later-stage only)

Opportunity: 1 (max. 1 initial market, 3 expansion)

Vision: 1 (an alternative is a roadmap slide)

Team: 1-2 (max. 2-sentence bios for each person)

Financials: 1 (more for later stage rounds)

Use of Funds: 1 (max. 3-5 spending buckets)

Why Now: 1 (max. 3 excellent reasons)

WRAPPING UP

We just learned a boatload of ways to improve your pitch deck.

We've *evaluated* your existing story using boosters, draggers, and their combined lift score.

We *elevated* the strength of your startup and focused your deck using the storyline compass and a linchpin vector.

And last, we *eliminated* the most common types of fluff from your pitch deck that would have detracted from its power.

I'll wrap things up with this: starting, launching, and building a business from the ground up is one of the most challenging things anyone can do. It's even harder when you don't have any capital to work with and are bootstrapping it from the ground up.

Investors and venture capitalists can be fantastic sources of growth capital and excellent partners in making the best decisions for your business.

Founders should view investors as long-term business partners. Even if an investor offers a term sheet, founders must carefully evaluate the deal and seek professional legal or financial advice when possible. Founders should also ask themselves if they want to work with that investor for the next five or more years. If you don't like an investor, just remember that you don't have to work with them. Partnerships are a two-way street.

On the other hand, if the investors seem like great people who would always act in the best interest of your company's success by providing you with the right resources to succeed *and* you get an outstanding term sheet, then rock 'n' roll.

It's your business, but success takes a village. Surround yourself with exceptional people who want to turn a dream into reality. Lastly, be open to new ideas and better ways of doing things from people who might be more experienced in areas you aren't.

Even if you only learned one new way to improve your pitch and hit your fundraising goals, I'll call that a win! Founders need to support one another, and an excellent way to do that is by recommending this book to others who may need it.

BEST OF LUCK FUNDRAISING!

KEANE ANGLE
FOUNDER
STORY PITCH DECKS

NEED MORE HELP?

Check out our in-house pitch deck research and articles:
storypitchdecks.com/articles

———

We've also got more downloads and courses for founders on our shop:
storypitchdecks.com/shop

STILL NEED HELP?

My company, STORY Pitch Decks, creates winning pitch decks
for startups all over the world.

We help with research, strategy, writing, and design.

To learn more about our services, head to **storypitchdecks.com**

www.ingramcontent.com/pod-product-compliance
Lightning Source LLC
Chambersburg PA
CBHW070535220526
45467CB00003B/955